The Memoirs of Napoleon, V11 1812

Louis Antoine Fauvelet de Bourrienne

Table of Contents

The Memoirs of Napoleon, V11, 1812..1
    Louis Antoine Fauvelet de Bourrienne..1
    CHAPTER XIX. 1809..2
    CHAPTER XX. 1809...6
    CHAPTER XXI. 1809..13
    CHAPTER XXII. 1809–1810...18
    CHAPTER XXIII. 1810...23
    CHAPTER XXIV. 1811...32
    CHAPTER XXV...37
    CHAPTER XXVI...49
    CHAPTER XXVII. 1812...61

The Memoirs of Napoleon, V11, 1812

Louis Antoine Fauvelet de Bourrienne

Kessinger Publishing reprints thousands of hard-to-find books!

Visit us at http://www.kessinger.net

- CHAPTER XIX. 1809.
- CHAPTER XX. 1809.
- CHAPTER XXI. 1809.
- CHAPTER XXII. 1809-1810.
- CHAPTER XXIII. 1810
- CHAPTER XXIV. 1811
- CHAPTER XXV.
- CHAPTER XXVI.
- CHAPTER XXVII. 1812.

```
MEMOIRS OF NAPOLEON BONAPARTE, VOLUME 11.

by LOUIS ANTOINE FAUVELET DE BOURRIENNE
His Private Secretary



Edited by R. W. Phipps
Colonel, Late Royal Artillery

1891
```

The Memoirs of Napoleon, V11, 1812

CHAPTER XIX. 1809.

```
The castle of Diernstein—Richard Coeur de Lion and Marshal Lannes,
—The Emperor at the gates of Vienna—The Archduchess Maria Louisa—
Facility of correspondence with England—Smuggling in Hamburg—Brown
sugar and sand—Hearses filled with sugar and coffee—Embargo on the
publication of news—Supervision of the 'Hamburg Correspondant'—
Festival of Saint Napoleon—Ecclesiastical adulation—The King of
Westphalia's journey through his States—Attempt to raise a loan—
Jerome's present to me—The present returned—Bonaparte's unfounded
suspicions.
```

Rapp, who during the campaign of Vienna had resumed his duties as aide de camp, related to me one of those observations of Napoleon which, when his words are compared with the events that followed them, seem to indicate a foresight into his future destiny. When within some days' march of Vienna the Emperor procured a guide to explain to him every village and ruin which he observed on the road. The guide pointed to an eminence on which were a few decayed vestiges of an old fortified castle. "Those," said the guide, "are the ruins of the castle of Diernstein." Napoleon suddenly stopped, and stood for some time silently contemplating the ruins, then turning to Lannes, who was with him, he raid, "See! yonder is the prison of Richard Coeur de Lion. He, like us, went to Syria and Palestine. But, my brave Lannes, the Coeur de Lion was not braver than you. He was more fortunate than I at St. Jean d'Acre. A Duke of Austria sold him to an Emperor of Germany, who imprisoned him in that castle. Those were the days of barbarism. How different from the civilisation of modern times! Europe has seen how I treated the Emperor of Austria, whom I might have made prisoner—and I would treat him so again. I claim no credit for this. In the present age crowned heads must be respected. A conqueror imprisoned!"

A few days after the Emperor was at the gates of Vienna, but on this occasion his access to the Austrian capital was not so easy as it had been rendered in 1805 by the ingenuity and courage of Lannes and Murat. The Archduke Maximilian, who was shut up in the capital, wished to defend it, although the French army already occupied the principal suburbs. In vain were flags of truce sent one after the other to the Archduke. They were not only dismissed unheard, but were even ill-treated, and one of them was almost killed by the populace. The city was then bombarded, and would speedily have been destroyed but that the Emperor, being informed that one of the Archduchesses remained in Vienna on account of ill-health, ordered the firing to cease. By a singular caprice of Napoleon's destiny this Archduchess was no other than Maria Louisa. Vienna at length opened her gates to Napoleon, who for some days took up his residence at Schoenbrunn.

The Emperor was engaged in so many projects at once that they could not all succeed. Thus, while he was triumphant in the Hereditary States his Continental system was experiencing severe checks. The trade with England on the coast of Oldenburg was carped on as uninterruptedly as if in time of peace. English letters and newspapers arrived on the Continent, and those of the Continent found their way into Great Britain, as if France and England had been united by ties of the firmest friendship. In short, things were just in the same state as if the decree for the blockade of the British Isles had not existed. When the custom-house officers succeeded in seizing contraband goods they were again taken from them by main force. On the 2d of July a serious contest took place at Brinskham between the custom-house officers and a party of peasantry, in which the latter remained masters of eighteen wagons laden with English goods: many were wounded on both sides.

If, however, trade with England was carried on freely along a vast extent of coast, it was different in the city of Hamburg, where English goods were introduced only by fraud; and I verily believe that the art of smuggling and the schemes of smugglers were never before carried to such perfection. Above 6000 persons of the lower orders went backwards and forwards, about twenty times a day, from Altona to Hamburg, and they carried on their contraband, trade by many ingenious stratagems, two of which were so curious that they are worth mentioning here.

On the left of the road leading from Hamburg to Altona there was a piece of ground where pits were dug for the purpose of procuring sand used for building and for laying down in the streets. At this time it was proposed to repair the great street of Hamburg leading to the gate of Altona. The smugglers overnight filled the sandpit with brown sugar, and the little carts which usually conveyed the sand into Hamburg were filled with the sugar, care being taken to cover it with a layer of sand about an inch thick. This trick was carried on for a length of time, but no progress was made in repairing the street. I complained greatly of the delay, even before I was aware of its cause, for the street led to a country-house I had near Altona, whither I went daily. The officers of the customs at length perceived that the work did not proceed, and one fine morning the sugar-carts were stopped and seized. Another expedient was then to be devised.

The Memoirs of Napoleon, V11, 1812

Between Hamburg and Altona there was a little suburb situated on the right bank of the Elbe. This suburb was inhabited, by sailors, labourers of the port, and landowners. The inhabitants were interred in the cemetery of Hamburg. It was observed that funeral processions passed this way more frequently than usual. The customhouse officers, amazed at the sudden mortality of the worthy inhabitants of the little suburb, insisted on searching one of the vehicles, and on opening the hearse it was found to be filled with sugar, coffee, vanilla, indigo, etc. It was necessary to abandon this expedient, but others were soon discovered.

Bonaparte was sensitive, in an extraordinary degree, to all that was said and thought of him, and Heaven knows how many despatches I received from headquarters during the campaign of Vienna directing me not only to watch the vigilant execution of the custom-house laws, but to lay an embargo on a thing which alarmed him more than the introduction of British merchandise, viz. the publication of news. In conformity with these reiterated instructions I directed especial attention to the management of the 'Correspondant'. The importance of this journal, with its 60,000 readers, may easily be perceived. I procured the insertion of everything I thought desirable: all the bulletins, proclamations, acts of the French Government, notes of the 'Moniteur', and the semi-official articles of the French journals: these were all given 'in extenso'. On the other hand, I often suppressed adverse news, which, though well known, would have received additional weight from its insertion in so widely circulated a paper. If by chance there crept in some Austrian bulletin, extracted from the other German papers published in the States of the Confederation of the Rhine, there was always given with it a suitable antidote to destroy, or at least to mitigate, its ill effect. But this was not all. The King of Wurtemberg having reproached the 'Correspondant', in a letter to the Minister for Foreign Affairs, with publishing whatever Austria wished should be made known, and being conducted in a spirit hostile to the good cause, I answered these unjust reproaches by making the Syndic censor prohibit the Hamburg papers from inserting any Austrian order of the day, any Archduke's bulletins, any letter from Prague; in short, anything which should be copied from the other German journals unless those articles had been inserted in the French journals.

My recollections of the year 1809 at Hamburg carry me back to the celebration of Napoleon's fete, which was on the 15th of August, for he had interpolated his patron saint in the Imperial calendar at the date of his birth. The coincidence of this festival with the Assumption gave rise to adulatory rodomontades of the most absurd description.

The Memoirs of Napoleon, V11, 1812

Certainly the Episcopal circulars under the Empire would form a curious collection.

> —[It will perhaps scarcely be believed that the following words were actually delivered from the pulpit: "God in his mercy has chosen Napoleon to be his representative on earth. The Queen of Heaven has marked, by the most magnificent of presents, the anniversary of the day which witnessed his glorious entrance into her domains. Heavenly Virgin! as a special testimony of your love for the French, and your all-powerful influence with your son, you have connected the first of your solemnities with the birth of the great Napoleon. Heaven ordained that the hero should spring from your sepulchre, —"Bourrienne.]—

Could anything be more revolting than the sycophancy of those Churchmen who declared that "God chose Napoleon for his representative upon earth, and that God created Bonaparte, and then rested; that he was more fortunate than Augustus, more virtuous than Trajan; that he deserved altars and temples to be raised to him!" etc.

Some time after the Festival of St. Napoleon the King of Westphalia made a journey through his States. Of all Napoleon's brothers the King of Westphalia was the one with whom I was least acquainted, and he, it is pretty well known, was the most worthless of the family. His correspondence with me is limited to two letters, one of which he wrote while he commanded the 'Epervier', and another seven years after, dated 6th September 1809. In this latter he said:

> "I shall be in Hannover on the 10th. If you can make it convenient to come there and spend a day with me it will give me great pleasure. I shall then be able to smooth all obstacles to the loan I wish to contract in the Hanse Town. I flatter myself you will do all in your power to forward that object, which at the present crisis is very important to my States. More than ample security is offered, but the money will be of no use to me if I cannot have it at least for two years."

Jerome wanted to contract at Hamburg a loan of 3,000,000 francs. However, the people did not seem to think like his Westphalian Majesty, that the contract presented more than ample security. No one was found willing to draw his purse-strings, and the loan was never raised.

Though I would not, without the Emperor's authority, exert the influence of my situation to further the success of Jerome's negotiation, yet I did my best to assist him. I succeeded in prevailing on the Senate to advance one loan of 100,000 francs to pay a portion of the arrears due to his troops, and a second of 200,000 francs to provide clothing for his army, etc. This scanty supply will cease to be wondered at when it is considered to what a state of desolation the whole of Germany was reduced at the time, as much in the allied States as in those of the enemies of France. I learnt at the time that the King of Bavaria said to an officer of the Emperor's household in whom he had great confidence, "If this continues we shall have to give up, and put the key under the door." These were his very words.

As for Jerome, he returned to Cassel quite disheartened at the unsuccessful issue of his loan. Some days after his return to his capital I received from him a snuffbox with his portrait set in diamonds, accompanied by a letter of thanks for the service I had rendered him. I never imagined that a token of remembrance from a crowned head could possibly be declined. Napoleon, however, thought otherwise. I had not, it is true, written to acquaint our Government with the King of Westphalia's loan, but in a letter, which I addressed to the Minister for Foreign Affairs on the 22d of September, I mentioned the present Jerome had sent me. Why Napoleon should have been offended at this I know not, but I received orders to return Jerome's present immediately, and these orders were accompanied with bitter reproaches for my having accepted it without the Emperor's authority. I sent back the diamonds, but kept the portrait. Knowing Bonaparte's distrustful disposition, I thought he must have suspected that Jerome had employed threats, or at any rate, that he had used some illegal influence to facilitate the success of his loan. At last, after much correspondence, Napoleon saw clearly that everything was perfectly regular; in a word, that the business had been transacted as between two private persons. As to the 300,000 francs which the Senate had lent to Jerome, the fact is, that but little scruple was made about it, for this simple reason, that it was the means of removing from Hamburg the Westphalian division, whose presence occasioned a much greater expense than the loan.

CHAPTER XX. 1809.

Visit to the field of Wagram.—Marshal Macdonald—Union of the Papal States with the Empire—The battle of Talavera—Sir Arthur Wellesley—English expedition to Holland—Attempt to assassinate the Emperor at Schoenbrunn—Staps Interrogated by Napoleon—Pardon

offered and rejected—Fanaticism and patriotism—Corvisart's
examination of Staps—Second interrogatory—Tirade against the
illuminati—Accusation of the Courts of Berlin and Weimar—Firmness
and resignation of Staps—Particulars respecting his death—
Influence of the attempt of Staps on the conclusion of peace—
M. de Champagny.

Napoleon went to inspect all the corps of his army and the field of Wagram, which a short time before had been the scene of one of those great battles in which victory was the more glorious in proportion as it had been valiantly contested.

—[The great battle of Wagram was fought on the 6th of July 1809.
The Austrians, who committed a mistake in over-extending their line,
lost 20,000 men as prisoners, besides a large number in killed and
wounded. There was no day, perhaps, on which Napoleon showed more
military genius or more personal courage. He was in the hottest of
the fight, and for a long time exposed to showers of grapeshot.-
Editor of 1836 edition.]—

On that day [the type] of French honour, Macdonald, who, after achieving a succession of prodigies, led the army of Italy into the heart of the Austrian States, was made a marshal on the field of battle. Napoleon said to him, "With us it is for life and for death." The general opinion was that the elevation of Macdonald added less to the marshal's military reputation than it redounded to the honour of the Emperor. Five days after the bombardment of Vienna, namely, on the 17th of May, the Emperor had published a decree, by virtue of which the Papal States were united to the French Empire, and Rome was declared an Imperial City. I will not stop to inquire whether this was good or bad in point of policy, but it was a mean usurpation on the part of Napoleon, for the time was passed when a Julius II. laid down the keys of St. Peter and took up the sword of St. Paul. It was, besides, an injustice, and, considering the Pope's condescension to Napoleon, an act of ingratitude. The decree of union did not deprive the Pope of his residence, but he was only the First Bishop of Christendom, with a revenue of 2,000,000.

Napoleon while at Vienna heard of the affair of Talavera de la Reyna. I was informed, by a letter from headquarters, that he was much affected at the news, and did not conceal his vexation. I verily believe that he was bent on the conquest of Spain, precisely on account of the difficulties he had to surmount. At Talavera commenced the celebrity of a man who, perhaps, would not have been without some glory even if pains had not been taken to build him up a great reputation. That battle commenced the career of Sir Arthur Wellesley, whose after-success, however, has been attended by such important consequences.

> —[The battle of Talavera took place on the 28th of July, twenty-two days after the fatal defeat of the Austrians at Wagram.]—

Whilst we experienced this check in Spain the English were attempting an expedition to Holland, where they had already made themselves masters of Walcheren. It is true they were obliged to evacuate it shortly after; but as at that time the French and Austrian armies were in a state of inaction, in consequence of the armistice concluded at Znaim, in Moravia, the news unfavourable to Napoleon had the effect of raising the hopes of the Austrian negotiators, who paused in the expectation that fresh defeats would afford them better chances.

It was during these negotiations, the termination of which seemed every day to be farther distant, that Napoleon was exposed to a more real danger than the wound he had received at Ratisbon. Germany was suffering under a degree of distress difficult to be described. Illuminism was making great progress, and had filled some youthful minds with an enthusiasm not less violent than the religious fanaticism to which Henry IV. fell a victim. A young man formed the design of assassinating Napoleon in order to rid Germany of one whom he considered her scourge. Rapp and Berthier were with the Emperor when the assassin was arrested, and in relating what I heard from them I feel assured that I am giving the most faithful account of all the circumstances connected with the event.

"We were at Schoenbrunn," said Rapp, "when the Emperor had just reviewed the troops. I observed a young man at the extremity of one of the columns just as the troops were about to defile. He advanced towards the Emperor, who was then between Berthier and me. The Prince de Neufchatel, thinking he wanted to present a petition, went forward to tell him that I was the person to receive it as I was the aide de camp for the day. The young man replied that he wished to speak with Napoleon himself, and Berthier again told him that he must apply to me. He withdrew a little, still repeating that he wanted to speak with Napoleon. He again advanced and came very near the Emperor; I desired him to fall back, telling him in German to wait till after the parade, when, if he had anything to say, it would be attended to. I surveyed him attentively, for I began to think his conduct suspicious. I observed that he kept his right hand in the breast pocket of his coat;

out of which a piece of paper appeared. I know not how it was, but at that moment my eyes met his, and I was struck with his peculiar look and air of fixed determination. Seeing an officer of gendarmerie on the spot, I desired him to seize the young man, but without treating him with any severity, and to convey him to the castle until the parade was ended.

All this passed in less time than I have taken to tell it, and as every one's attention was fixed on the parade the scene passed unnoticed. I was shortly afterwards told that a large carving-knife had been found on the young man, whose name was Staps. I immediately went to find Duroc, and we proceeded together to the apartment to which Staps had been taken. We found him sitting on a bed, apparently in deep thought, but betraying no symptoms of fear. He had beside him the portrait of a young female, his pocket-book, and purse containing only two pieces of gold. I asked him his name, but he replied that he would tell it to no one but Napoleon. I then asked him what he intended to do with the knife which had been found upon him? But he answered again, 'I shall tell only Napoleon.'—'Did you mean to attempt his life?'—`Yes.'—` Why?'—`I can tell no one but Napoleon.'

"This appeared to me so strange that I thought right to inform the Emperor of it. When I told him what had passed he appeared a little agitated, for you know how he was haunted with the idea of assassination. He desired that the young man should be taken into his cabinet; whither he was accordingly conducted by two gens d'armes. Notwithstanding his criminal intention there was something exceedingly prepossessing in his countenance. I wished that he would deny the attempt; but how was it possible to save a man who was determined to sacrifice himself? The Emperor asked Staps whether he could speak French, and he answered that he could speak it very imperfectly, and as you know (continued Rapp) that next to you I am the best German scholar in Napoleon's Court, I was appointed interpreter on this occasion. The Emperor put the following questions to Staps, which I translated, together with the answers:

"`Where do you come from?'—'From Narremburgh.'—`What is your father?' —`A Protestant minister.'—`How old are you?'—'Eighteen.'—'What did you intend to do with your knife?'—`To kill you.'—'You are mad, young man; you are one of the illuminati?'—'I am not mad; I know not what is meant by the illuminati!'—'You are ill, then?'—'I am not; I am very well.'—'Why did you wish to kill me?'—'Because you have ruined my country.'—'Have I done you any harm?'—'Yes, you have harmed me as well as

The Memoirs of Napoleon, V11, 1812

all Germans.'—'By whom were you sent? Who urged you to this crime?' —'No one; I was urged to it by the sincere conviction that by killing you I should render the greatest service to my country.'—'Is this the first time you have seen me?'—'I saw you at Erfurt, at the time of your interview with the Emperor of Russia.'—'Did you intend to kill me then?'—'No; I thought you would not again wage war against Germany. I was one of your greatest admirers.'—'How long have you been in Vienna?' —'Ten days.'—'Why did you wait so long before you attempted the execution of your project?'—'I came to Schoenbrunn a week ago with the intention of killing you, but when I arrived the parade was just over; I therefore deferred the execution of my design till today.'—'I tell you, young man, you are either mad or in bad health.'

"The Emperor here ordered Corvisart to be sent for. Staps asked who Corvisart was? I told him that he was a physician. He then said, 'I have no need of him.' Nothing further was said until the arrival of the doctor, and during this interval Steps evinced the utmost indifference. When Corvisart arrived Napoleon directed him to feel the young man's pulse, which he immediately did; and Staps then very coolly said, 'Am I not well, sir?' Corvisart told the Emperor that nothing ailed him. 'I told you so,' said Steps, pronouncing the words with an air of triumph.

"I was really astonished at the coolness and apathy of Staps, and the Emperor seemed for a moment confounded by the young man's behaviour. — After a few moments' pause the Emperor resumed the interrogatory as follows:

"`Your brain is disordered. You will be the ruin of your family. I will grant you your life if you ask pardon for the crime you meditated, and for which you ought to be sorry.'—'I want no pardon. I only regret having failed in my attempt.'—'Indeed! then a crime is nothing to you?' —'To kill you is no crime: it is a duty.'—'Whose portrait is that which was found on you?'—'It is the portrait of a young lady to whom I am attached.'—'She will doubtless be much distressed at your adventure?'— 'She will only be sorry that I have not succeeded. She abhors you as much as I do.'—'But if I were to pardon you would you be grateful for my mercy?'—'I would nevertheless kill you if I could.'

"I never," continued Rapp, "saw Napoleon look so confounded. The replies of Staps and his immovable resolution perfectly astonished him. He ordered the prisoner to be removed; and when he was gone Napoleon said, 'This is the result of the secret societies which infest Germany. This is the effect of fine principles and the light of reason. They make young men assassins. But what can be done against illuminism? A sect cannot be destroyed by cannon-balls.'

"This event, though pains were taken to keep it secret, became the subject of conversation in the castle of Schoenbrunn. In the evening the Emperor sent for me and said, 'Rapp, the affair of this morning is very extraordinary. I cannot believe that this young man of himself conceived the design of assassinating me. There is something under it. I shall never be persuaded that the intriguers of Berlin and Weimar are strangers to the affair.'—'Sire, allow me to say that your suspicions appear unfounded. Staps has had no accomplice; his placid countenance, and even his fanaticism, are easiest proofs of that.'—'I tell you that he has been instigated by women: furies thirsting for revenge. If I could only obtain proof of it I would have them seized in the midst of their Court.'—'Ah, Sire, it is impossible that either man or woman in the Courts of Berlin or Weimar could have conceived so atrocious a design.'— 'I am not sure of that. Did not those women excite Schill against us while we were at peace with Prussia; but stay a little; we shall see.'— 'Schill's enterprise; Sire, bears no resemblance to this attempt.' You know how the Emperor likes every one to yield to his opinion when he has adopted one which he does not choose to give up; so he said, rather changing his tone of good-humoured familiarity, 'All you say is in vain, Monsieur le General: I am not liked either at Berlin or Weimar.' There is no doubt of that, Sire; but because you are not liked in these two Courts, is it to be inferred that they would assassinate you?'—'I know the fury of those women; but patience. Write to General Lauer: direct him to interrogate Staps. Tell him to bring him to a confession.'

"I wrote conformably with the Emperor's orders, but no confession was obtained from Staps. In his examination by General Lauer he repeated nearly what he had said in the presence of Napoleon. His resignation and firmness never forsook him for a moment; and he persisted in saying that he was the sole author of the attempt, and that no one else was aware of it. Staps' enterprise made a deep impression on the Emperor. On the day when we left Schoenbrunn we happened to be alone, and he said to me, 'I cannot get this unfortunate Staps out of my mind. The more I think on the subject the more I am perplexed. I never can believe that a young man of his age, a German, one who has received a good education, a Protestant too, could have conceived and attempted such a crime. The Italians are said to be a nation of assassins, but no Italian ever attempted my life. This affair is beyond my comprehension. Inquire how Staps died, and let me know.'

The Memoirs of Napoleon, V11, 1812

"I obtained from General Lauer the information which the Emperor desired. I learned that Staps, whose attempt on the Emperor's life was made on the 23d of October; was executed at seven o'clock in the morning of the 27th, having refused to take any sustenance since the 24th. When any food was brought to him he rejected it, saying, 'I shall be strong enough to walk to the scaffold.' When he was told that peace was concluded he evinced extreme sorrow, and was seized with trembling. On reaching the place of execution he exclaimed loudly, 'Liberty for ever! Germany for ever! Death to the tyrant!'"

Such are the notes which I committed to paper after conversing with Rapp, as we were walking together in the garden of the former hotel of Montmorin, in which Rapp resided. I recollect his showing me the knife taken from Staps, which the Emperor had given him; it was merely a common carving-knife, such as is used in kitchens. To these details may be added a very remarkable circumstance, which I received from another but not less authentic source. I have been assured that the attempt of the German Mutius Scaevola had a marked influence on the concessions which the Emperor made, because he feared that Staps, like him who attempted the life of Porsenna, might have imitators among the illuminati of Germany.

It is well known that after the battle of Wagram conferences were open at Raab. Although peace was almost absolutely necessary for both powers, and the two Emperors appeared to desire it equally, it was not, however, concluded. It is worthy of remark that the delay was occasioned by Bonaparte. Negotiations were therefore suspended, and M. de Champagny had ceased for several days to see the Prince of Lichtenstein when the affair of Staps took place. Immediately after Napoleon's examination of the young fanatic he sent for M. de Champagny: "How are the negotiations going on?" he inquired. The Minister having informed him, the Emperor added, "I wish them to be resumed immediately: I wish for peace; do not hesitate about a few millions more or less in the indemnity demanded from Austria. Yield on that point. I wish to come to a conclusion: I refer it all to you." The Minister lost no time in writing to the Prince of Lichtenstein: on the same night the two negotiators met at Raab, and the clauses of the treaty which had been suspended were discussed, agreed upon, and signed that very night. Next morning M. de Champagny attended the Emperor's levee with the treaty of peace as it had been agreed on. Napoleon, after hastily examining it, expressed his approbation of every particular, and highly complimented his Minister on the speed with which the treaty had been brought to a conclusion.'

—[This definitive treaty of peace, which is sometimes called the Treaty of Vienna, Raab, or Schoenbrunn, contained the following articles:

1. Austria ceded in favour of the Confederation of the Rhine (these fell to Bavaria), Salzburg, Berchtolsgaden, and a part of Upper Austria.

2. To France directly Austria ceded her only seaport, Trieste, and all the countries of Carniola, Friuli, the circle of Vilach, with parts of Croatia end Dalmatia. (By these cessions Austria was excluded from the Adriatic Sea, and cut off from all communication with the navy of Great Britain.) A small lordship, en enclave in the, territories of the Grieve League, was also gives up.

3. To the constant ally of Napoleon, to the King of Saxony, in that character Austria ceded some Bohemian enclaves in Saxony end, in his capacity of Grand Duke of Warsaw, she added to his Polish dominions the ancient city of Cracow, and all Western Galicia.

4. Russia, who had entered with but a lukewarm zeal into the war as an ally of France, had a very moderate share of the spoils of Austria. A portion of Eastern Galicia, with a population of 400,000 souls, was allotted to her, but in this allotment the trading town of Brody (almost the only thing worth having) was specially excepted. This last circumstance gave no small degree of disgust to the Emperor Alexander, whose admiration of Napoleon was not destined to have a long duration, —Editor of 1836 edition.

CHAPTER XXI. 1809.

The Princess Royal of Denmark—Destruction of the German Empire—Napoleons visit to the Courts of Bavaria and Wurtemberg—His return to France—First mention of the divorce—Intelligence of Napoleon's marriage with Maria Louisa—Napoleon's quarrel with Louis—Journey of the Emperor and Empress into Holland—Refusal of the Hanse Towns to pay the French troops—Decree for burning English merchandise—M. de Vergennes—Plan for turning an inevitable evil to the best account—Fall on the exchange of St Petersburg

About this time I had the pleasure of again seeing the son of the reigning Duke of Mecklenburg-Schwerin, whose arrival in the Hanse Towns was speedily followed by that of his sister, Princess Frederica Charlotte of Mecklenburg, married to the Prince Royal of Denmark, Christian Frederick. In November the Princess arrived at Altana from Copenhagen, the reports circulated respecting her having compelled her husband to separate from her. The history of this Princess, who, though perhaps blamable, was nevertheless much pitied, was the general subject of conversation in the north of Germany at the time I was at Hamburg. The King of Denmark, grieved at the publicity of the separation, wrote a letter on the subject to the Duke of Mecklenburg. In this letter, which I had an opportunity of seeing, the King expressed his regret at not having been able to prevent the scandal; for, on his return from a journey to Kiel, the affair had become so notorious that all attempts at reconciliation were vain. In the meantime it was settled that the Princess was to remain at Altona until something should be decided respecting her future condition.

It was Baron Plessen, the Duke of Mecklenburg's Minister of State, who favoured me with a sight of the King of Denmark's letters. M. Plessen told me, likewise, at the time that the Duke had formed the irrevocable determination of not receiving his daughter. A few days after her arrival the Princess visited Madame de Bourrienne. She invited us to her parties, which were very brilliant, and several times did us the honour of being present at ours. But; unfortunately, the extravagance of her conduct, which was very unsuitable to her situation, soon became the subject of general animadversion.

I mentioned at the close of the last chapter how the promptitude of M. de Champagny brought about the conclusion of the treaty known by the name of the Treaty of Schoenbrunn. Under this the ancient edifice of the German Empire was overthrown, and Francis II. of Germany became Francis I., Emperor of Austria. He, however, could not say, like his namesake of France, 'Tout est perdu fors l'honneur'; for honour was somewhat committed, even had nothing else been lost. But the sacrifices Austria was compelled, to make were great. The territories ceded to France were immediately united into a new general government, under the collective denomination of the Illyrian Provinces. Napoleon thus became master of both sides of the Adriatic, by virtue of his twofold title of Emperor of France and King of Italy. Austria, whose external commerce thus received a check, had no longer any direct communication with the sea. The loss of Fiume, Trieste, and the sea-coast appeared so vast a sacrifice that it was impossible to look forward to the duration of a peace so dearly purchased.

The Memoirs of Napoleon, V11, 1812

The affair of Staps, perhaps, made Napoleon anxious to hurry away from Schoenbrunn, for he set off before he had ratified the preliminaries of the peace, announcing that he would ratify them at Munich. He proceeded in great haste to Nymphenburg, where he was expected on a visit to the Court of Bavaria. He next visited the King of Wurtemberg, whom he pronounced to be the cleverest sovereign in Europe, and at the end of October he arrived at Fontainebleau. From thence he proceeded on horseback to Paris, and he rode so rapidly that only a single chasseur of his escort could keep up with him, and, attended by this one guard, he entered the court of the Tuileries. While Napoleon was at Fontainebleau, before his return to Paris, Josephine for the first time heard the divorce mentioned; the idea had occurred to the Emperor's mind while he was at Schoenbrunn. It was also while at Fontainebleau that Napoleon appointed M. de Montalivet to be Minister of the Interior. The letters which we received from Paris at this period brought intelligence of the brilliant state of the capital during the winter of 1809, and especially of the splendour of the Imperial Court, where the Emperor's levees were attended by the Kings of Saxony, Bavaria, and Wurtemberg, all eager to evince their gratitude to the hero who had raised them to the sovereign rank.

I was the first person in Hamburg who received intelligence of Napoleon's projected marriage with the Archduchess Maria Louisa. The news was brought to me from Vienna by two estafettes. It is impossible to describe the effect produced by the anticipation of this event throughout the north of Germany.

```
-["Napoleon often reflected on the best mode of making this
communication to the Empress; still he was reluctant to speak to
her.  He was apprehensive of the consequences of her susceptibility
of feeling; his heart was never proof against the shedding of tears.
Ho thought, however, that a favourable opportunity offered for
breaking the subject previously to his quitting Fontainebleau.  He
hinted at it in a few words which bc had addressed to the Empress,
but he did not explain himself until the arrival of the viceroy,
whom he had ordered to join him.  He was the first person who spoke
openly to his mother and obtained her consent for that bitter
sacrifice.  He acted on the occasion like a kind son and a man
grateful to his benefactor and devoted to his service, by sparing
him the necessity of unpleasant explanations towards a partner whose
removal was a sacrifice as painful to him as it was affecting: The
Emperor, having arranged whatever related to the future condition of
the Empress, upon whom he made a liberal settlement, urged the
moment of the dissolution of the marriage, no doubt because he felt
```

> grieved at the condition of the Empress herself, who dined every day and passed her evenings in the presence of persons who were witnessing her descent from the throne. There existed between him and the Empress Josephine no other bond than a civil act, according to the custom which prevailed at the time of this marriage. Now the law had foreseen the dissolution of such marriage oontracts. A particular day having therefore been fixed upon, the Emperor brought together into his apartments those persons whose ministry was required in this case; amongst others, the Arch-Chancellor and M. Regnault de St. Jean d'Angely. The Emperor then declared in a loud voice his intention of annulling the marriage he had contracted with Josephine, who was present; the Empress also made the same declaration, which was interrupted by her repeated sobs. The Prince Arch-Chancellor having caused the article of the law to be read, he applied it to the cam before him, and declared the marriage to be dissolved " (Memoirs of ad Due de Rovigo).]—

From all parts the merchants received orders to buy Austrian stock, in which an extraordinary rise immediately took place. Napoleon's marriage with Maria Louisa was hailed with enthusiastic and general joy. The event was regarded as the guarantee of a long peace, and it was hoped there would be a lasting cessation of the disasters created by the rivalry of France and Austria. The correspondence I received showed that these sentiments were general in the interior of France, and in different countries of Europe; and, in spite of the presentiments I had always had of the return of the Bourbons to France, I now began to think that event problematic, or at least very remote.

About the beginning of the year 1810 commenced the differences between Napoleon and his brother Louis, which, as I have already stated, ended in a complete rupture. Napoleon's object was to make himself master of the navigation of the Scheldt which Louis wished should remain free, and hence ensued the union of Holland with the French Empire. Holland was the first province of the Grand Empire which Napoleon took the new Empress to visit. This visit took place almost immediately after the marriage. Napoleon first proceeded to Compiegne, where he remained a week. He next set out for St. Quentin, and inspected the canal. The Empress Maria Louisa then joined him, and they both proceeded to Belgium. At Antwerp the Emperor inspected all the works which he had ordered, and to the execution of which he attached great importance. He returned by way of Ostend, Lille, and Normandy to St. Cloud, where he arrived on the 1st of June 1810. He there learned from my correspondence that the Hanse Towns—refused to advance money for the pay of the French troops. The men were absolutely destitute. I declared that it was urgent to put an end to this state of things. The Hanse towns had been reduced from opulence to misery by taxation and exactions, and were no longer able to provide the funds.

During this year Napoleon, in a fit of madness, issued a decree which I cannot characterise by any other epithet than infernal. I allude to the decree for burning all the English merchandise in France, Holland, the Grand Duchy of Berg, the Hanse Towns; in short, in all places subject to the disastrous dominion of Napoleon. In the interior of France no idea could possibly be formed of the desolation caused by this measure in countries which existed by commerce; and what a spectacle was it to, the, destitute inhabitants of those countries to witness the destruction of property which, had it been distributed, would have assuaged their misery!

Among the emigrants whom I was ordered to watch was M. de Vergennes, who had always remained at or near Hamburg Since April 1808. I informed the Minister that M. de Vergennes had presented himself to me at this time. I even remember that M. de Vergennes gave me a letter from M. de Remusat, the First Chamberlain of the Emperor. M. de Remusat strongly recommended to me his connection, who was called by matters of importance to Hamburg. Residence in this town was, however, too expensive, and he decided to live at Neumuhl, a little village on the Elbe, rather to the west of Altona. There he lived quietly in retirement with an opera dancer named Mademoiselle Ledoux, with whom he had become acquainted in Paris, and whom he had brought with him. He seemed much taken with her. His manner of living did not denote large means.

One duty with which I was entrusted, and to which great importance was attached, was the application and execution of the disastrous Continental system in the north. In my correspondence I did not conceal the dissatisfaction which this ruinous measure excited, and the Emperor's eyes were at length opened on the subject by the following circumstance. In spite of the sincerity with which the Danish Government professed to enforce the Continental system, Holstein contained a great quantity of colonial produce; and, notwithstanding the measures of severity, it was necessary that that merchandise should find a market somewhere. The smugglers often succeeded in introducing it into Germany, and the whole would probably soon have passed the custom-house limits. All things considered, I thought it advisable to make the best of an evil that could not be avoided. I therefore proposed that the colonial produce then in Holstein, and which had been imported before the date of the King's edict for its prohibition, should be allowed to enter Hamburg on the payment of 30, and on some articles 40, per cent. This duty was to be collected at the custom-house, and was to be confined entirely to articles consumed in Germany. The colonial produce in Altona, Glnckstadt, Husum, and other towns of Holstein, lead been estimated, at about 30,000,000 francs, and the duty would amount to 10,000,000 or 12,000,000. The adoption of the plan I proposed would naturally put a stop to smuggling; for it could not be doubted that the merchants would give 30 or 33 per cent for the right of carrying on a lawful trade rather than give 40 per cent. to the smugglers, with the chance of seizure.

The Emperor immediately adopted my idea, for I transmitted my suggestions to the Minister for Foreign Affairs on the 18th of September, and on the 4th of October a decree was issued conformable to the plan I proposed. Within six weeks after the decree came into operation the custom-house Director received 1300 declarations from persons holding colonial produce in Holstein. It now appeared that the duties would amount to 40,000,000 francs, that is to say, 28,000,000 or 30,000,000 more than my estimate.

Bernadotte had just been nominated Prince Royal of Sweden. This nomination, with all the circumstances connected with it, as well as Bernadotte's residence in Hamburg, before he proceeded to Stockholm, will be particularly noticed in the next chapter. I merely mention the circumstance here to explain some events which took place in the north, and which were, more or less, directly connected with it. For example, in the month of September the course of exchange on St. Petersburg suddenly fell. All the letters which arrived in Hamburg from the capital of Russia and from Riga, attributed the fall to the election of the Prince of Ponte-Corvo as Prince Royal of Sweden. Of thirty letters which I received there was not one but described the consternation which the event had created in St. Petersburg. This consternation, however, might have been excited less by the choice of Sweden than by the fear that that choice was influenced by the French Government.

CHAPTER XXII. 1809–1810.

```
Bernadotte elected Prince Royal of Sweden-Count Wrede's overtures
to Bernadotte-Bernadottes's three days' visit to Hamburg-
Particulars respecting the battle of Wagram-Secret Order of the
day-Last intercourse of the Prince Royal of Sweden with Napoleon-
My advice to Bernadotte respecting the Continental system.
```

The Memoirs of Napoleon, V11, 1812

I now come to one of the periods of my life to which I look back with moat satisfaction, the time when Bernadotte was with me in Hamburg. I will briefly relate the series of events which led the opposer of the 18th Brumaire to the throne of Sweden.

On the 13th of march 1809 Gustavus Adolphus was arrested, and his uncle, the Duke of Sudermania, provisionally took the reins of Government. A few days afterwards Gustavus published his act of abdication, which in the state of Sweden it was impossible for him to refuse. In May following, the Swedish Diet having been convoked at Stockholm, the Duke of Sudermania was elected King. Christian Augustus, the only son of that monarch, of course became Prince Royal on the accession of his father to the throne. He, however, died suddenly at the end of May 1810, and Count Fersen (the same who at the Court of Marie Antoinette was distinguished by the appellation of 'le beau Fersen'), was massacred by the populace, who suspected, perhaps unjustly, that he had been accessory to the Prince's death.

```
—[Count Fereen, alleged to have been one of the favoured lovers of
Marie Antoinette, and who was certainly deep in her confidence, had
arranged most of the details of the attempted flight to Varennes in
1791, and he himself drove the Royal family their first stage to the
gates of Paris.]—
```

On the 21st of August following Bernadotte was elected Prince Royal of Sweden.

After the death of the Prince Royal the Duke of Sudermania's son, Count Wrede, a Swede, made the first overtures to Bernadotte, and announced to him the intention entertained at Stockholm of offering him the throne of Sweden. Bernadotte was at that time in Paris, and immediately after his first interview with Count Wrede he waited on the Emperor at St. Cloud; Napoleon coolly replied that he could be of no service to him; that events must take their course; that he might accept or refuse the offer as he chose; that he (Bonaparte) would place no obstacles in his way, but that he could give him no advice. It was very evident that the choice of Sweden was not very agreeable to Bonaparte, and though he afterwards disavowed any opposition to it, he made overtures to Stockholm, proposing that the crown of Sweden should be added to that of Denmark.

Bernadotte then went to the waters of Plombieres, and on his return to Paris he sent me a letter announcing his elevation to the rank of Prince Royal of Sweden.

The Memoirs of Napoleon, V11, 1812

On the 11th of October he arrived in Hamburg, where he stayed only three days. He passed nearly the whole of that time with me, and he communicated to me many curious facts connected with the secret history of the times, and among other things some particulars respecting the battle of Wagram. I was the first to mention to the new Prince Royal of Sweden the reports of the doubtful manner in which the troops under his command behaved. I reminded him of Bonaparte's dissatisfaction at these troops; for there was no doubt of the Emperor being the author of the complaints contained in the bulletins, especially as he had withdrawn the troops from Bernadotte's command. Bernadotte assured me that Napoleon's censure was unjust; during the battle he had complained of the little spirit manifested by the soldiers. "He refused to see me," added Bernadotte, "and I was told, as a reason for his refusal, that he was astonished and displeased to find that, notwithstanding his complaints, of which I must have heard, I had boasted of having gained the battle, and had publicly complimented the Saxons whom I commanded."

Bernadotte then showed me the bulletin he drew up after the battle of Wagram. I remarked that I had never heard of a bulletin being made by any other than the General who was Commander-in-Chief during a battle, and asked how the affair ended. He then handed to me a copy of the Order of the day, which Napoleon said he had sent only to the Marshals commanding the different corps.

Bernadotte's bulletin was printed along with Bonaparte's Order of the Day, a thing quite unparalleled.

Though I was much interested in this account of Bonaparte's conduct after the battle of Wagram; yet I was more curious to hear the particulars of Bernadotte's last communication with the Emperor. The Prince informed me that on his return from Plombieres he attended the levee, when the Emperor asked him, before every one present, whether he had received any recent news from Sweden.

He replied in the affirmative. "What is it?" inquired Napoleon. "Sire, I am informed that your Majesty's charge d'afaires at Stockholm opposes my election. It is also reported to those who choose to believe it that your Majesty gives the preference to the King of Denmark."—"At these words," continued Bernadotte, "the Emperor affected surprise, which you know he can do very artfully. He assured me it was impossible, and then turned the conversation to another subject.

The Memoirs of Napoleon, V11, 1812

"I know not what to think of his conduct in this affair. I am aware he does not like me;—but the interests of his policy may render him favourable to Sweden. Considering the present greatness and power of France, I conceived it to be my duty to make every personal sacrifice. But I swear to Heaven that I will never commit the honour of Sweden. He, however, expressed himself in the best possible terms in speaking of Charles XIII. and me. He at first started no obstacle to my acceptance of the succession to the throne of Sweden, and he ordered the official announcement of my election to be immediately inserted in the Moniteur'. Ten days elapsed without the Emperor's saying a word to me about my departure. As I was anxious to be off, and all my preparations were made, I determined to go and ask him for the letters patent to relieve me from my oath of fidelity, which I had certainly kept faithfully in spite of all his ill-treatment of me. He at first appeared somewhat surprised at my request, and, after a little hesitation, he said, 'There is a preliminary condition to be fulfilled; a question has been raised by one of the members of the Privy Council.'—'What condition, Sire?'—'You must pledge yourself not to bear arms against me.'—'Does your Majesty suppose that I can bind myself by such an engagement? My election by the Diet of Sweden, which has met with your Majesty's assent, has made me a Swedish subject, and that character is incompatible with the pledge proposed by a member of the Council. I am sure it could never have emanated from your Majesty, and must proceed from the Arch-Chancellor or the Grand Judge, who certainly could not have been aware of the height to which the proposition would raise me.'—'What do you mean?'—'If, Sire, you prevent me accepting a crown unless I pledge myself not to bear arms against you, do you not really place me on a level with you as a General?'

"When I declared positively that my election must make me consider myself a Swedish subject he frowned, and seemed embarrassed. When I had done speaking he said, in a low and faltering voice, 'Well, go. Our destinies will soon be accomplished!' These words were uttered so indistinctly that I was obliged to beg pardon for not having heard what. he said, and he repented, 'Go! our destinies will soon be accomplished!' In the subsequent conversations which I had with the Emperor I tried all possible means to remove the unfavourable sentiments he cherished towards me. I revived my recollections of history. I spoke to him of the great men who had excited the admiration of the world, of the difficulties and obstacles which they had to surmount; and, above all, I dwelt upon that solid glory which is founded on the establishment and maintenance of public tranquillity and happiness. The Emperor listened to me attentively, and frequently concurred in my opinion as to the principles of the prosperity and stability of States. One day he took my hand and pressed it affectionately, as if to assure me of his friendship and protection. Though I knew him to be an adept in the art of dissimulation, yet his affected kindness appeared so natural that I thought all his unfavourable feeling towards me was at an end. I spoke to persons by whom our two families were allied, requesting that they would assure the Emperor of the reciprocity of my sentiments, and tell him that I was ready to assist his great plans in any way not hostile to the interests of Sweden.

"Would you believe, my dear friend, that the persons to whom I made these candid protestations laughed at my credulity? They told me that after the conversation in which the Emperor had so cordially pressed my hand. I had scarcely taken leave of him when he was heard to say that I had made a great display of my learning to him, and that he had humoured me like a child. He wished to inspire me with full confidence so as to put me off my guard; and I know for a certainty that he had the design of arresting me.

"But," pursued Bernadotte, "in spite of the feeling of animosity which I know the Emperor has cherished against me since the 18th Brumaire, I do not think, when once I shall be in Sweden, that he will wish to have any differences with the Swedish Government. I must tell you, also be has given me 2,000,000 francs in exchange for my principality of Ponte−Corvo. Half the sum has been already paid, which will be very useful to me in defraying the expenses of my journey and installation. When I was about to step into my carriage to set off, an individual, whom you must excuse me naming, came to bid me farewell, and related to me a little conversation which had just taken place at the Tuileries. Napoleon said to the individual in question, 'Well, does not the Prince regret leaving France?'—'Certainly, Sire.'—'As to me, I should have been very glad if he had not accepted his election. But there is no help for it . . . . He does not like me.'—'Sire, I must take the liberty of saying that your Majesty labours under a mistake. I know the differences which have existed between you and General Bernadotte for the last six years. I know how he opposed the overthrow of the Directory; but I also know that the Prince has long been sincerely attached to you.'—'Well, I dare say you are right. But we have not understood each other. It is now too late. He has his interests and his policy, and I have mine.'"

"Such," added the Prince, "were the Emperor's last observations respecting me two hours before my departure. The individual to whom I have just alluded, spoke truly, my dear Bourrienne. I am indeed sorry to leave France; and I never should have left it but for the injustice of Bonaparte. If ever I ascend the throne of Sweden I shall owe my crown to his ill-treatment of me; for had he not persecuted me by his animosity my condition would have sufficed for a soldier of fortune: but we must follow our fate."

During the three days the Prince spent with me I had many other conversations with him. He wished me to give him my advice as to the course he should pursue with regard to the Continental system. "I advise you," said I, "to reject the system without hesitation. It may be very fine in theory, but it is utterly impossible to carry it into practice, and it will, in the end, give the trade of the world to England. It excites the dissatisfaction of our allies, who, in spite of themselves, will again become our enemies. But no other country, except Russia, is in the situation of Sweden. You want a number of objects of the first necessity, which nature has withheld from you. You can only obtain them by perfect freedom of navigation; and you can only pay for them with those peculiar productions in which Sweden abounds. It would be out of all reason to close your ports against a nation who rules the seas. It is your navy that would be blockaded, not hers. What can France do against you? She may invade you by land. But England and Russia will exert all their efforts to oppose her. By sea it is still more impossible that she should do anything. Then you have nothing to fear but Russia and England, and it will be easy for you to keep up friendly relations with these two powers. Take my advice; sell your iron, timber, leather, and pitch; take in return salt, wines, brandy, and colonial produce. This is the way to make yourself popular in Sweden. If, on the contrary, you follow the Continental system, you will be obliged to adopt laws against smuggling, which will draw upon you the detestation of the people."

Such was the advice which I gave to Bernadotte when he was about to commence his new and brilliant career. In spite of my situation as a French Minister I could not have reconciled it to my conscience to give him any other counsel, for if diplomacy has duties so also has friendship. Bernadotte adopted my advice, and the King of Sweden had no reason to regret having done so.

CHAPTER XXIII. 1810

```
Bernadotte's departure from Hamburg—The Duke of Holstein-
Augustenburg—Arrival of the Crown Prince in Sweden—
Misunderstandings between him and Napoleon—Letter from Bernadotte
to the Emperor—Plot for kidnapping the Prince Royal of Sweden—
Invasion of Swedish Pomerania—Forced alliance of Sweden with
England and Russia—Napoleon's overtures to Sweden—Bernadotte's
```

letters of explanation to the Emperor—The Princess Royal of Sweden—My recall to Paris—Union of the Hanse Towns with France—Dissatisfaction of Russia—Extraordinary demand made upon me by Bonaparte—Fidelity of my old friends—Duroc and Rapp—Visit to Malmaison, and conversation with Josephine.

While Bernadotte was preparing to fill the high station to which he had been called by the wishes of the people of Sweden, Napoleon was involved in his misunderstanding with the Pope,

—[It was about this time that, irritated at what he called the captive Pope's unreasonable obstinacy, Bonaparte conceived, and somewhat openly expressed, his notion of making France s Protestant country, and changing the religion of 30,000,000 of people by an Imperial decree. One or two of the good sayings of the witty, accomplished, and chivalrous Comte Louis de Narbonne have already been given in the course of these volumes. The following is another of them:

"I tell yon what I will do, Narbonne—I tell you how I will vent my spite on this old fool of a Pope, and the dotards who may succeed him said Napoleon one day at the Tuileries. "I will make a schism as great as that of Luther—I will make France a Protestant country!"

"O Sire," replied the Count, "I see difficulties in the way of this project. In the south, in the Vendee, in nearly all the west, the French are bigoted Catholics and even what little religion remains among us in our cities and great towns is of the Roman Church."

"Never mind, Narbonne—never mind!—I shall at least carry a large portion of the French people with me—I will make a division!" Sire, replied Narbonne, "I am afraid that there is not enough religion in all France to stand division!"-Editor of 1836 edition.]—

and in the affairs of Portugal, which were far from proceeding according to his wishes. Bernadotte had scarcely quitted Hamburg for Sweden when the Duke of Holstein-Augustenburg arrived. The Duke was the brother of the last Prince Royal of Sweden, whom Bernadotte was called to succeed, and he came to escort his sister from Altona to Denmark. His journey had been retarded for some days on account of the presence of the Prince of Ponte-Gorvo in Hamburg: the preference granted to Bernadotte had mortified his ambition, and he was unwilling to come in contact with his fortunate rival. The Duke was favoured, by the Emperor of Russia.

As soon as he arrived in Sweden Bernadotte directed his aide de camp, General Lentil de St. Alphonse, to inform me of his safe passage. Shortly after I received a letter from Bernadotte himself, recommending one of his aides de camp, M. Villatte, who was the bearer of it. This letter contained the same sentiments of friendship as those I used to receive from General Bernadotte, and formed a contrast with the correspondence of King Jerome, who when he wrote to me assumed the regal character, and prayed that God would have me in his holy keeping. However, the following is the Prince Royal's letter:

> MY DEAR BOURRIENNE—I have directed M. Villatte to see you on his way through Hamburg, and to bear my friendly remembrances to you. Lentil has addressed his letter to you, which I suppose you have already received. Adieu, care for me always, and believe in the inalterable attachment of yours,
>
> (Signed) CHARLES JOHN.
>
> P.S.—I beg yon will present my compliments to madame and all your family. Embrace my little cousin for me.

The little cousin, so called by Bernadotte, was one of my daughters, then a child, whom Bernadotte used to be very fond of while he was at Hamburg.

Departing from the order of date, I will anticipate the future, and relate all I know respecting the real causes of the misunderstanding which arose between Bernadotte and Napoleon. Bonaparte viewed the choice of the Swedes with great displeasure, because he was well aware that Bernadotte had too much integrity and honour to serve him in the north as a political puppet set in motion by means of springs which he might pull at Paris or at his headquarters. His dissatisfaction upon this point occasioned an interesting correspondence, part of which, consisting of letters from Bernadotte to the Emperor, is in my possession. The Emperor had allowed Bernadotte to retain in his service, for a year at least, the French officers who were his aides de camp—but that permission was soon revoked, end the Prince Royal of Sweden wrote to Napoleon a letter of remonstrance.

Napoleon's dissatisfaction with the Prince Royal now changed to decided resentment. He repented having acceded to his departure from France, and he made no secret of his sentiments, for he said before his courtiers, "That he would like to send Bernadotte to Vincennes to finish his study of the Swedish language." Bernadotte was informed of this, but he could not believe that the Emperor had ever entertained such a design. However, a conspiracy was formed in Sweden against Bernadotte, whom a party of foreign brigands were hired to kidnap in the neighbourhood of Raga; but the plot was discovered, and the conspirators were compelled to embark without their prey. The Emperor having at the same time seized upon Swedish Pomerania, the Prince Royal wrote him a second letter in these terms:

```
From the papers which have just arrived I learn that a division of
the army, under the command of the Prince of Eckmuhl, invaded
Swedish Pomerania on the night of the 26th of January; that the
division continued to advance, entered the capital of the Duchy, and
took possession of the island of Rugen.  The King expects that your
Majesty will explain the reasons which have induced you to act in a
manner so contrary to the faith of existing treaties.  My old
connection with your Majesty warrants me in requesting you to
declare your motives without delay, in order that I may give my
advice to the King as to the conduct which Sweden ought hereafter to
adopt.  This gratuitous outrage against Sweden is felt deeply by the
nation, and still more, Sire, by me, to whom is entrusted the honour
of defending it.  Though I have contributed to the triumphs of
France, though I have always desired to see her respected and happy;
yet I can never think of sacrificing the interests, honour, and
independence of the country which has adopted me.  Your Majesty, who
has so ready a perception of what is just, must admit the propriety
of my resolution.  Though I am not jealous of the glory and power
which surrounds you, I cannot submit to the dishonour of being
regarded as a vassal.  Your Majesty governs the greatest part of
Europe, but your dominion does not extend to the nation which I have
been called to govern; my ambition is limited to the defence of
Sweden.  The effect produced upon the people by the invasion of
which I complain may lead to consequences which it is impossible to
foresee; and although I am not a Coriolanus, and do not command the
Volsci, I have a sufficiently good opinion of the Swedes to assure
you that they dare undertake anything to avenge insults which they
have not provoked, and to preserve rights to which they are as much
attached as to their lives.
```

I was in Paris when the Emperor received Bernadotte's letter on the occupation of Swedish Pomerania. When Bonaparte read it I was informed that he flew into a violent rage, and even exclaimed, "You shall submit to your degradation, or die sword in hand!" But his rage was impotent. The unexpected occupation of Swedish Pomerania obliged the King of Sweden to come to a decided rupture with France, and to seek other allies, for Sweden was not strong enough in herself to maintain neutrality in the midst of the general conflagration of Europe after the disastrous campaign of Moscow. The Prince Royal, therefore, declared to Russia and England that in consequence of the unjust invasion of Pomerania Sweden was at war with France, and he despatched Comte de Lowenhjelm, the King's aide de camp, with a letter explanatory of his views. Napoleon sent many notes to Stockholm, where M. Alquier, his Ambassador, according to his instructions, had maintained a haughty and even insulting tone towards Sweden. Napoleon's overtures, after the manifestations of his anger, and after the attempt to carry off the Prince Royal, which could be attributed only to him, were considered by the Prince Royal merely as a snare. But in the hope of reconciling the duties he owed to both his old and his new country he addressed to the Emperor a moderate letter:

This letter throws great light on the conduct of the Emperor with respect to Bernadotte; for Napoleon was not the man whom any one whatever would have ventured to remind of facts, the accuracy of which was in the least degree questionable. Such then were the relations between Napoleon and the Prince Royal of Sweden. When I shall bring to light some curious secrets, which have hitherto been veiled beneath the mysteries of the Restoration, it will be seen by what means Napoleon, before his fall, again sought to wreak his vengeance upon Bernadotte.

Oh the 4th of December I had the honour to see the Princess Royal of Sweden, —[Madame Bernadotte, afterwards Queen of Sweden, was a Mademoiselle Clary, and younger sister to the wife of Joseph Bonaparte]— who arrived that day at Hamburg. She merely passed through the city on her way to Stockholm to join her husband, but she remained but a short time in Sweden, —two months, I believe, at most, not being able to reconcile herself to the ancient Scandinavia. As to the Prince Royal, he soon became inured to the climate, having been for many years employed in the north.

After this my stay at Hamburg was not of long duration. Bonaparte's passion for territorial aggrandisement knew no bounds; and the turn of the Hanse Towns now arrived. By taking possession of these towns and territories he merely accomplished a design formed long previously. I, however, was recalled with many compliments, and under the specious pretext that the Emperor wished to hear my opinions respecting the

The Memoirs of Napoleon, V11, 1812

country in which. I had been residing. At the beginning of December I received a letter from M. de Champagny stating that the Emperor wished to see me in order to consult with me upon different things relating to Hamburg. In this note I was told "that the information I had obtained respecting Hamburg and the north of Germany might be useful to the public interest, which must be the most gratifying reward of my labours." The reception which awaited me will presently be seen. The conclusion of the letter spoke in very flattering terms of the manner in which I had discharged my duties. I received it on the 8th of December, and next day I set out for Paris. When I arrived at Mayence I was enabled to form a correct idea of the fine compliments which had been paid me, and of the Emperor's anxiety to have my opinion respecting the Hanse Towns. In Mayence I met the courier who was proceeding to announce the union of the Hanse Towns with the French Empire. I confess that, notwithstanding the experience I had acquired of Bonaparte's duplicity, or rather, of the infinite multiplicity of his artifices, he completely took me by surprise on that occasion.

On my arrival in Paris I did not see the Emperor, but the first 'Moniteur' I read contained the formula of a 'Senatus-consulte,' which united the Hanse Towns, Lauenburg, etc., to the French Empire by the right of the strongest. This new and important augmentation of territory could not fail to give uneasiness to Russia. Alexander manifested his dissatisfaction by prohibiting the importation of our agricultural produce and manufactures into Russia. Finally, as the Continental system had destroyed all trade by the ports of the Baltic, Russia showed herself more favourable to the English, and gradually reciprocal complaints of bad faith led to that war whose unfortunate issue was styled by M. Talleyrand "the beginning of the end."

I have now to make the reader acquainted with an extraordinary demand made upon me by the Emperor through the medium of M. de Champagny. In one of my first interviews with that Minister after my return to Paris he thus addressed me: "The Emperor has entrusted me with a commission to you which I am obliged to execute: 'When you see Bourrienne,' said the Emperor, 'tell him I wish him to pay 6,000,000 into your chest to defray the expense of building the new Office for Foreign Affairs.'" I was so astonished at this unfeeling and inconsiderate demand that I was utterly unable to make airy reply. This then was my recompense for having obtained money and supplies during my residence at Hamburg to the extent of nearly 100,000,000, by which his treasury and army had profited in moments of difficulty! M. de Champagny added that the Emperor did not wish to receive me. He asked what answer he should bear to his Majesty. I still remained silent, and the Minister again urged me to give an answer. "Well, then," said I, "tell him he may go to the devil." The Minister naturally wished to obtain some variation from this laconic answer, but I would give no other; and I afterwards learned from Duroc that M. de Champagny was compelled to communicate it to Napoleon. "Well," asked the latter, "have you seen Bourrienne?"—"Yes, Sire."—"Did you tell him I wished him to pay 6,000,000 into your chest?"—" Yes, Sire."—"And what did he say?"—" Sire, I dare not inform your Majesty."—"What did he say? I insist upon knowing."—"Since you insist on my telling you, Sire, M. de Bourrienne said your Majesty might go to- the devil."—"Ah! ah! did he really say so?" The Emperor then retired to the recess of a window, where he remained alone for seven or eight minutes, biting his nails; in the fashion of Berthier, and doubtless giving free scope to his projects of vengeance. He then turned to the Minister and spoke to him of quite another subject: Bonaparte had so nursed himself in the idea of making me pay the 6,000,000 that every time he passed the Office for Foreign Affairs he said to those who accompanied hint; "Bourrienne must pay for that after all."

```
—[This demand of money from Bourrienne is explained in Erreurs
(tome ii, p.  228) by the son of Davoust.  Bourrienne had been
suspected by Napoleon of making large sums at Hamburg by allowing
breaches of the Continental system.  In one letter to Davoust
Napoleon speaks of an " immense fortune," and in another, that
Bourrienne is reported to have gained seven or eight millions at
Hamburg in giving licences or making arbitrary seizures.]—
```

Though I was not admitted to the honour of sharing the splendour of the Imperial Court; yet I had the satisfaction of finding that; in spite of my disgrace, those of my old friends who were worth anything evinced the same regard for me as heretofore. I often saw Duroc; who snatched some moments from his more serious occupations to come and chat with me respecting all that had occurred since my secession from Bonaparte's cabinet. I shall not attempt to give a verbatim account of my conversations with Duroc, as I have only my memory to guide me; but I believe I shall not depart from the truth in describing them as follows:

On his return from the last Austrian campaign Napoleon; as I have already stated, proceeded to Fontainebleau, where he was joined by Josephine. Then, for the first time, the communication which had always existed between the apartments of the husband and wife was closed. Josephine was fully alive to the fatal prognostics which were to be deduced from this conjugal separation. Duroc informed me that she sent for him, and on entering her chamber, he found her bathed in tears. "I am lost!" she exclaimed in a tone of voice the remembrance of which seemed sensibly to affect Duroc even while relating the circumstance to me: "I am utterly lost! all is over now! You, Duroc, I know, have always been my friend, and so has Rapp. It is not you who have persuaded him to part from me. This is the work of my enemies Savary and Junot! But they are more his enemies than mine. And my poor Eugene I how will he be distressed when he learns I am repudiated by an ungrateful man! Yes Duroc, I may truly call him ungrateful, My God! my God! what will become of us?" . . . Josephine sobbed bitterly while she thus addressed Duroc.

Before I was acquainted with the singular demand which M. de Champagny was instructed to make to me I requested Duroc to inquire of the Emperor his reason for not wishing to see me. The Grand Marshal faithfully executed my commission, but he received only the following answer: "Do you think I have nothing better to do than to give Bourrienne an audience? that would indeed furnish gossip for Paris and Hamburg. He has always sided with the emigrants; he would be talking to me of past times; he was for Josephine! My wife, Duroc, is near her confinement; I shall have a son, I am sure!.... Bourrienne is not a man of the day; I have made giant strides since he left France; in short, I do not want to see him. He is a grumbler by nature; and you know, my dear Duroc, I do not like men of that sort."

I had not been above a week in Paris when Duroc related this speech to me. Rapp was not in France at the time, to my great regret. Much against his inclination he had been appointed to some duties connected with the Imperial marriage ceremonies, but shortly after, having given offence to Napoleon by some observation relating to the Faubourg St. Germain, he had received orders to repair to Dantzic, of which place he had already been Governor.

The Emperor's refusal to see me made my situation in Paris extremely delicate; and I was at first in doubt whether I might seek an interview with Josephine. Duroc, however, having assured me that Napoleon would have no objection to it, I wrote requesting permission to wait upon her. I received an answer the same day, and on the morrow I repaired to Malmaison. I was ushered into the tent drawing-room, where I found Josephine and Hortense. When I entered Josephine stretched out her hand to me, saying, "Ah! my friend!" These words she pronounced with deep emotion, and tears prevented her from continuing. She threw herself on the ottoman on the left of the fireplace, and beckoned me to sit down beside her. Hortense stood by the fireplace, endeavouring to conceal her tears. Josephine took my hand, which she pressed in both her own; and, after a struggle to overcome her feelings, she said, " My dear Bourrienne, I have drained my cup of misery. He has cast me off! forsaken me! He conferred upon me the vain title of Empress only to render my fall the more marked. Ah! we judged him rightly! I knew the destiny that awaited me; for what would he not sacrifice to his ambition!" As she finished these words one of Queen Hortense's ladies entered with a message to her; Hortense stayed a few moments, apparently to recover from the emotion under which she was labouring, and then withdrew, so that I was left alone with Josephine. She seemed to wish for the relief of disclosing her sorrows, which I was curious to hear from her own lips; women have such a striking way of telling their distresses. Josephine confirmed what Duroc had told me respecting the two apartments at Fontainebleau; then, coming to the period when Bonaparte had declared to her the necessity of a separation, she said, °° My dear Bourrienne; during all the years you were with us you know I made you the confidant of my thoughts, and kept you acquainted with my sad forebodings. They are now cruelly fulfilled. I acted the part of a good wife to the very last. I have suffered all, and I am resigned! . . . What fortitude did it require latterly to endure my situation, when, though no longer his wife, I was obliged to seem so in the eyes of the world! With what eyes do courtiers look upon a repudiated wife! I was in a state of vague uncertainty worse than death until the fatal day when he at length avowed to me what I had long before read in his looks! On the 30th of November 1809 we were dining together as usual, I had not uttered a word during that sad dinner, and he had broken silence only to ask one of the servants what o'clock it was. As soon as Bonaparte had taken his coffee he dismissed all the attendants, and I remained alone with him. I saw in the expression of his countenance what was passing in his mind, and I knew that my hour was come. He stepped up to me—he was trembling, and I shuddered; he took my hand, pressed it to his heart, and after gazing at me for a few moments in silence he uttered these fatal words: 'Josephine! my dear Josephine! You know how I have loved you! . . . To you, to you alone, I owe the only moments of happiness I have tasted in this world. But, Josephine, my destiny is not to be controlled by my will. My dearest affections must yield to the interests of France.'—'Say no more,' I exclaimed, 'I understand you; I expected this, but the blow is not the less mortal.' I could not say another word," continued Josephine; "I know not what happened after I seemed to lose my reason; I became insensible, and when I recovered I found myself in my chamber. Your friend Corvisart and my poor daughter were with me. Bonaparte came to see me in the evening; and oh! Bourrienne, how can I describe to you what I felt at the sight of him; even the interest he evinced for me seemed an additional cruelty. Alas! I had good reason to fear ever becoming an Empress!"

I knew not what consolation to offer: to Josephine; and knowing as I did the natural lightness of her character, I should have been surprised to find her grief so acute, after the lapse of a year, had I not been aware that there are certain chords which, when struck, do not speedily cease to vibrate in the heart of a woman. I sincerely pitied Josephine, and among all the things I said to assuage her sorrow, the consolation to which she appeared most sensible was the reprobation which public opinion had pronounced on Bonaparte's divorce, and on this subject I said nothing but the truth, for Josephine was generally beloved. I reminded her of a prediction I had made under happier circumstances, viz. on the day that she came to visit us in our little house at Ruel. "My dear friend," said she, "I have not forgotten it, and I have often thought of all you then said. For my part, I knew he was lost from the day he made himself Emperor. Adieu! Bourrienne, come and see me soon again; come often, for we have a great deal to talk about; you know how happy I always am to see you." Such was, to the best of my recollection, what passed at my first interview with Josephine after my return from Hamburg.

CHAPTER XXIV. 1811

>Arrest of La Sahla—My visit to him—His confinement at Vincennes—Subsequent history of La Sahla—His second journey to France—Detonating powder—Plot hatched against me by the Prince of Eckmuhl—Friendly offices of the Due de Rovigo—Bugbears of the police—Savary, Minister of Police.

I had been in Paris about two months when a young man of the name of La Sahla was arrested on the suspicion of having come from Saxony to attempt the life of the Emperor. La Sahla informed the Duo de Rovigo, then Minister of the Police, that he wished to see me, assigning as a reason for this the reputation I had left behind me in Germany. The Emperor, I presume, had no objection to the interview, for I received an invitation to visit the prisoner. I accordingly repaired to the branch office of the Minister of the Police, in the Rue des St. Peres, where I was introduced to a young man between seventeen and eighteen years of age.

My conversation with the young man, whose uncle was, I believe, Minister to the King of

The Memoirs of Napoleon, V11, 1812

Saxony, interested me greatly in his behalf; I determined, if possible, to save La Sahla, and I succeeded. I proceeded immediately to the Duo de Rovigo, and I convinced him that under the circumstances of the case it was important to make it be believed that the young man was insane. I observed that if he were brought before a court he would repeat all that he had stated to me, and probably enter into disclosures which might instigate fresh attempts at assassination. Perhaps an avenger of La Sahla might rise up amongst the students of Leipzig, at which university he had spent his youth. These reasons, together with others, had the success I hoped for. The Emperor afterwards acknowledged the prudent course which had been adopted respecting La Sahla; when speaking at St. Helena of the conspiracies against his life he said, "I carefully concealed all that I could."

In conformity with my advice La Sahla was sent to Vincennes, where he remained until the end of March 1814, He was then removed to the castle of Saumur, from which he was liberated at the beginning of April. I had heard nothing of him for three years, when one day, shortly after the Restoration, whilst sitting at breakfast with my family at my house in the Rue Hauteville, I heard an extraordinary noise in the antechamber, and before I had time to ascertain its cause I found myself in the arms. of a young man, who embraced me with extraordinary ardour. It was La Sahla. He was in a transport of gratitude and joy at his liberation, and at the accomplishment of the events which he had wished to accelerate by assassination. La Sahla returned to Saxony and I saw no more of him, but while I was in Hamburg in 1815, whither I was seat by Louis XVIII., I learned that on the 5th of June a violent explosion was heard in the Chamber of Representatives at Paris, which was at first supposed to be a clap of thunder, but was soon ascertained to have been occasioned by a young Samson having fallen with a packet of detonating powder in his pocket.

On receiving this intelligence I imagined, I know not why, that this young Saxon was La Sahla, and that he had probably intended to blow up Napoleon and even the Legislative Body; but I have since ascertained that I was under a mistake as to his intentions. My knowledge of La Sahla's candour induces me to believe the truth of his declarations to the police; and if there be any inaccuracies in the report of these declarations I do not hesitate to attribute them to the police itself, of which Fouche was the head at the period in question.

It is the latter part of the report which induced me to observe above, that if there were any inaccuracies in the statement they were more likely to proceed from Fouche's police than the false representations of young La Sahla. It is difficult to give credit without proof to such accusations. However, I decide nothing; but I consider it my duty to express doubts of the truth of these charges brought against the two Prussian ministers, of whom the Prince of Wittgenstein, a man of undoubted honour, has always spoken to me in the best of terms.

There is nothing to prove that La Sahla returned to France the second time with the same intentions as before. This project, however, is a mystery to me, and his detonating powder gives rise to many conjectures.

I had scarcely left Hamburg when the Prince of Eckmuhl (Marshal Davoust) was appointed Governor–General of that place on the union of the Hanse Towns with the Empire. From that period I was constantly occupied in contending against the persecutions and denunciations which he racked his imagination to invent. I cannot help attributing to those persecutions the Emperor's coolness towards me on my arrival in Paris. But as Davoust's calumnies were devoid of proof, he resorted to a scheme by which a certain appearance of probability might supply the place of truth. When I arrived in Paris, at the commencement of 1811, I was informed by an excellent friend I had left at Hamburg, M. Bouvier, an emigrant, and one of the hostages of Louis XVI., that in a few days I would receive a letter which would commit me, and likewise M. de Talleyrand and General Rapp. I had never had any connection on matters of business, with either of these individuals, for whom I entertained the most sincere attachment. They, like myself, were not in the good graces of Marshal Davoust, who could not pardon the one for his incontestable superiority of talent, and the other for his blunt honesty. On the receipt of M. Bouvier's letter I carried it to the Due de Rovigo, whose situation made him perfectly aware of the intrigues which had been carried on against me since I had left Hamburg by one whose ambition aspired to the Viceroyalty of Poland. On that, as on many other similar occasions, the Duc de Rovigo advocated my cause with Napoleon. We agreed that it would be best to await the arrival of the letter which M. Bouvier had announced. Three weeks elapsed, and the letter did not appear. The Duc de Rovigo, therefore, told me that I must have been misinformed. However, I was certain that M. Bouvier would not have sent me the information on slight grounds, and I therefore supposed that the project had only been delayed. I was not wrong in my conjecture, for at length the letter arrived. To what a depth of infamy men can descend! The. letter was from a man whom I had known at Hamburg, whom I had obliged, whom I had employed as a spy. His epistle was a miracle of impudence. After relating some extraordinary transactions which he said had taken place between us, and which all bore the stamp of falsehood, he requested me to send him by return of post the sum of 60,000 francs on account of what I had promised him for some business he executed in England by the direction of M. de Talleyrand, General Rapp, and myself. Such miserable wretches are often caught in the snares they spread for others. This was the case in the present instance, for the fellow had committed, the blunder of fixing upon the year 1802 as the period of this pretended business in England, that is to say, two years before my appointment as Minister-Plenipotentiary to the Hanse Towns. This anachronism was not the only one I discovered in the letter.

I took a copy of the letter, and immediately carried the original to the Duc de Rovigo, as had been agreed between us. When I waited on the Minister he was just preparing to go to the Emperor. He took with him the letter which I brought, and also the letter which announced its arrival. As the Duc de Rovigo entered the audience-chamber Napoleon advanced to meet him, and apostrophised him thus: "Well, I have learned fine things of your Bourrienne, whom you are always defending." The fact was, the Emperor had already received a copy of the letter, which had been opened at the Hamburg post-office. The Due de Rovigo told the Emperor that he had long known what his Majesty had communicated to him. He then entered into a full explanation of the intrigue, of which it was wished to render me the victim, and proved to him the more easily the falsehood of my accusers by reminding him that in 1802 I was not in Hamburg, but was still in his service at home.

It may be supposed that I was too much interested in knowing what had passed at the Tuileries not to return to the Duc de Rovigo the same day. I learned from him the particulars which I have already related. He added that he had observed to the Emperor that there was no connection between Rapp and M. Talleyrand which could warrant the suspicion of their being concerned in the affair in question. "When Napoleon saw the matter in its true light," said Savary, "when I proved to him the palpable existence of the odious machination, he could not find terms to express his indignation. 'What baseness, what horrible villainy!' he exclaimed; and gave me orders to arrest and bring to Paris the infamous writer of the letter; and you may rely upon it his orders shall be promptly obeyed."

Savary, as he had said, instantly despatched orders for the arrest of the writer, whom he directed to be sent to France. On his arrival he was interrogated respecting the letter. He declared that he had written it at the instigation and under the dictation of Marshal Davoust, for doing which he received a small sum of money as a reward. He also confessed that when the letter was put into the post the Prince of Eckmuhl ordered the Director of the Post to open it, take a copy, then seal it again, and send it to its address—that is to say, to me—and the copy to the Emperor. The writer of the letter was banished to Marseilles, or to the Island of Hyeres, but the individual who dictated it continued a Marshal, a Prince, and a Governor-General, and still looked forward to the Viceroyalty of Poland! Such was the discriminating justice of the Empire; and Davoust continued his endeavours to revenge himself by other calumnies for my not having considered him a man of talent. I must do the Duc de Rovigo the justice to say that, though his fidelity to Napoleon was as it always had been, boundless, yet whilst he executed the Emperor's orders he endeavoured to make him acquainted with the truth, as was proved by his conduct in the case I have just mentioned. He was much distressed by the sort of terror which his appointment had excited in the public, and he acknowledged to me that he intended to restore confidence by a more mild system than that of his predecessor. I had observed formerly that Savary did not coincide in the opinion I had always entertained of Fouche, but when once the Due de Rovigo endeavoured to penetrate the labyrinth of police, counter-police, inspections and hierarchies of espionage, he found they were all bugbears which Fouche had created to alarm the Emperor, as gardeners put up scarecrows among the fruit-trees to frighten away the sparrows. Thus, thanks to the artifices of Fouche, the eagle was frightened as easily as the sparrows, until the period when the Emperor, convinced that Fouche was maintaining a correspondence with England through the agency of Ouvrard, dismissed him.

I saw with pleasure that Savary, the Minister of Police, wished to simplify the working of his administration, and to gradually diminish whatever was annoying in it, but, whatever might be his intentions, he was not always free to act. I acknowledge that when I read his Memoirs I saw with great impatience that in many matters he had voluntarily assumed responsibilities for acts which a word from him might have attributed to their real author. However this may be, what much pleased me in Savary was the wish he showed to learn the real truth in order to tell it to Napoleon. He received from the Emperor more than one severe rebuff. This came from the fact that since the immense aggrandisement of the Empire the ostensible Ministers, instead of rising in credit, had seen their functions diminish by degrees. Thus proposals for appointments to the higher grades of the army came from the cabinet of Berthier, and not from that of the Minister-of-War. Everything which concerned any part of the government of the Interior or of the Exterior, except for the administration of War and perhaps for that of Finance, had its centre in the cabinet of M. Maret, certainly an honest man, but whose facility in saying "All is right," so much helped to make all wrong.

The home trade, manufactures, and particularly several of the Parisian firms were in a state of distress the more hurtful as it contrasted so singularly with the splendour of the Imperial Court since the marriage of Napoleon with Maria Louisa. In this state of affairs a chorus of complaints reached the ears of the Duc de Rovigo every day. I must say that Savary was never kinder to me than since my disgrace; he nourished my hope of getting Napoleon to overcome the prejudices against me with which the spirit of vengeance had inspired him, and I know for certain that Savary returned to the charge more than once to manage this. The Emperor listened without anger, did not blame him for the closeness of our intimacy, and even said to him some obliging but insignificant words about me. This gave time for new machinations against me, and to fill him with fresh doubts when he had almost overcome his former, ideas.

CHAPTER XXV.

```
M. Czernischeff—Dissimulation of Napoleon—Napoleon and Alexander—
Josephine's foresight respecting the affairs of Spain—My visits to
Malmaison—Grief of Josephine—Tears and the toilet—Vast extent of
the Empire—List of persons condemned to death and banishment in
Piedmont—Observation of Alfieri respecting the Spaniards—Success
in Spain—Check of Massena in Portugal—Money lavished by the
English—Bertrand sent to Illyria, and Marmont to Portugal—
Situation of the French army—Assembling of the Cortes—Europe
sacrificed to the Continental system—Conversation with Murat in the
Champs Elysees—New titles and old names—Napoleon's dislike of
literary men—Odes, etc., on the marriage of Napoleon—Chateaubriand
and Lemereier—Death of Chenier—Chateaubriand elected his successor
—His discourse read by Napoleon—Bonaparte compared to Nero—
Suppression of the 'Merceure'—M. de Chateaubriand ordered to leave
Paris—MM. Lemercier and Esmenard presented to the Emperor—Birth of
the King of Rome—France in 1811.
```

Since my return to France I had heard much of the intrigues of M. Czernischeff, an aide de camp of the Emperor of Russia, who, under the pretest of being frequently sent to compliment Napoleon on the part of the Emperor Alexander, performed, in fact, the office of a spy. The conduct of Napoleon with regard to M. Czernischeff at that period struck me as singular, especially after the intelligence which before my departure from

The Memoirs of Napoleon, V11, 1812

Hamburg I had transmitted to him respecting the dissatisfaction of Russia and her hostile inclinations. It is therefore clear to me that Bonaparte was well aware of the real object of M. Czernischeffs mission, and that if he appeared to give credit to the increasing professions of his friendship it was only because he still wished, as he formerly did; that Russia might so far commit herself as to afford him a fair pretext for the commencement, of hostilities in the north.

M. Czernischeff first arrived in Paris shortly after the interview at Erfurt, and after that period was almost constantly on the road between Paris and St. Petersburg; it has been computed that in the space of less than four years he travelled more than 10,000 leagues. For a long time his frequent journeyings excited no surmises, but while I was in Paris Savary began to entertain suspicions, the correctness of which it was not difficult to ascertain, so formidable was still the system of espionage, notwithstanding the precaution taken by Fouche to conceal from his successor the names of his most efficient spies. It was known that M. Czernischeff was looking out for a professor of mathematics,—doubtless to disguise the real motives for his stay in Paris by veiling them under the desire of studying the sciences. The confidant of Alexander had applied to a professor connected with a public office; and from that time all the steps of M. Czermseheff were known to the police. It was discovered that he was less anxious to question his instructor respecting the equations of a degree, or the value of unknown quantities, than to gain all the information he could about the different branches of the administration, and particularly the department of war. It happened that the professor knew some individuals employed in the public offices, who furnished him with intelligence, which he in turn communicated to M. Czernischeff, but not without making a report of it to the police; according to custom, instead of putting an end to this intrigue at once it was suffered fully to develop itself. Napoleon was informed of what was going on, and in this instance gave a new proof of his being an adept in the art of dissimulation, for, instead of testifying any displeasure against M. Czernischeff, he continued to receive him with the same marks of favour which he had shown to him during his former missions to Paris. Being, nevertheless, desirous to get rid of him, without evincing a suspicion that his clandestine proceedings had been discovered, he entrusted him with a friendly letter to his brother of Russia, but Alexander was in such haste to reply to the flattering missive of his brother of France that M. Czernischeff was hurried back to Paris, having scarcely been suffered to enter the gates of St. Petersburg. I believe I am correct in the idea that Napoleon was not really displeased at the intrigues of M. Czernischeff, from the supposition that they afforded an indication of the hostile intentions of Russia towards

The Memoirs of Napoleon, V11, 1812

France; for, whatever he might say on this subject to his confidants, what reliance can we place on the man who formed the camp of Boulogne without the most distant intention of attempting a descent upon England, and who had deceived the whole world respecting that important affair without taking any one into his own confidence?

During the period of my stay in Paris the war with Spain and Portugal occupied much of the public attention; and it proved in the end an enterprise upon which the intuition of Josephine had not deceived her. In general she intermeddled little with political affairs; in the first place, because her doing so would have given offence to Napoleon; and next, because her natural frivolity led her to give a preference to lighter pursuits. But I may safely affirm that she was endowed with an instinct so perfect as seldom to be deceived respecting the good or evil tendency of any measure which Napoleon engaged in; and I remember she told me that when informed of the intention of the Emperor to bestow the throne of Spain on Joseph, she was seized with a feeling of indescribable alarm. It would be difficult to define that instinctive feeling which leads us to foresee the future; but it is a fact that Josephine was endowed with this faculty in a more perfect decree than any other person I have ever known, and to her it was a fatal gift, for she suffered at the same time under the weight of present and of future misfortunes.

I often visited her at Malmaison, as Duroc assured me that the Emperor had no objection to my doing so; yet he must have been fully aware that when Josephine and I were in confidential conversation he would not always be mentioned in terms of unqualified eulogy; and in truth, his first friend and his first wife might well be excused for sometimes commingling their complaints.

Though more than a twelvemonth had elapsed since the divorce grief still preyed on the heart of Josephine. "You cannot conceive, my friend," she often said to me, "all the torments that I have suffered since that fatal day! I cannot imagine how I survived it. You cannot figure to yourself the pain I endure on seeing descriptions of his fetes everywhere. And the first time he came to visit me after his marriage, what a meeting was that! How many tears I shed! The days on which he comes are to me days of misery, for he spares me not. How cruel to speak of his expected heir. Bourrienne, you cannot conceive how heart-rending all this is to me! Better, far better to be exiled a thousand leagues from hence! However," added Josephine, "a few friends still remain faithful in my changed fortune, and that is now the only thing which affords me even temporary consolation." The truth is that she was extremely unhappy, and the most acceptable consolation her friends could offer her was to weep with her. Yet such was still Josephine's passion for dress, that after. having wept for a quarter of an hour she would dry her tears to give audience to milliners and jewellers. The sight of a new hat would call forth all Josephine's feminine love of finery. One day I remember that, taking advantage of the momentary serenity occasioned by an ample display of sparkling gewgaws, I congratulated her upon the happy influence they exercised over her spirits, when she said, "My dear friend, I ought, indeed, to be indifferent to all this; but it is a habit." Josephine might have added that it was also an occupation, for it would be no exaggeration to say that if the time she wasted in tears and at her toilet had been subtracted from her life its duration would have been considerably shortened.

The vast extent of the French Empire now presented a spectacle which resembled rather the dominion of the Romans and the conquests of Charlemagne than the usual form and political changes of modern Europe. In fact, for nearly two centuries, until the period of the Revolution, and particularly until the elevation of Napoleon, no remarkable changes had taken place in the boundaries of European States, if we except the partition of Poland, when two of the co-partitioners committed the error of turning the tide of Russia towards the west! Under Napoleon everything was overturned with astonishing rapidity: customs, manners, laws, were superseded

> —[The so-called "French" armies of the time, drawn from all parts of the Empire and from the dependent States, represented the extraordinary fusion attempted by Napoleon. Thus, at the battle of Ocana there were at least troops of the following States, viz. Warsaw, Holland, Baden, Nassau, Hesse-Darmstadt, Frankfort, besides the Spaniards in Joseph's service. A Spanish division went to Denmark, the regiment from Isembourg was sent to Naples, while the Neapolitans crossed to Spain. Even the little Valais had to furnish a battalion. Blacks from San Domingo served in Naples, while sixteen nations, like so many chained dogs, advanced into Russia. Such troops could not have the spirit of a homogeneous army.
>
> Already, in 1808, Metternich had written from Paris to his Court, "It is no longer the nation that fights: the present war (Spain) is Napoleon's war; it is not even that of his army." But Napoleon himself was aware of the danger of the Empire from its own extent. In the silence of his cabinet his secretary Meneval sometimes heard him murmur, "L'arc est trop longtemps tendu."]—

by new customs, new manners, and new laws, imposed by force, and forming a heterogeneous whole, which could not fail to dissolve, as soon as the influence of the power which had created it should cease to operate. Such was the state of Italy that I have been informed by an individual worthy of credit that if the army of Prince Eugene, instead of being victorious, had been beaten on the Piava, a deeply-organised revolution would have broken out in Piedmont, and even in the Kingdom of Italy, where, nevertheless, the majority of the people fully appreciated the excellent qualities of Eugene. I have been also credibly informed that lists were in readiness designating those of the French who were to be put to death, as well as those by whom the severe orders of the Imperial Government had been mitigated, and who were only to be banished. In fact, revolt was as natural to the Italians as submission to the Germans, and as the fury of despair to the Spanish nation. On this subject I may cite an observation contained in one of the works of Alfieri, published fifteen years before the Spanish war. Taking a cursory view of the different European nations he regarded—the Spaniards as the only people possessed of "sufficient energy to struggle against foreign usurpation." Had I still been near the person of Napoleon I would most assuredly have resorted to an innocent artifice, which I had several times employed, and placed the work of Alfieri on his table open at the page I wished him to read. Alfieri's opinion of the Spanish people was in the end fully verified; and I confess I cannot think without shuddering of the torrents of blood which inundated the Peninsula; and for what? To make Joseph Bonaparte a King!

The commencement of 1811 was sufficiently favourable to the French arms in Spain, but towards the beginning of March the aspect of affairs changed. The Duke of Belluno, notwithstanding the valour of his troops, was unsuccessful at Chiclana; and from that day the French army could not make head against the combined forces of England and Portugal. Even Massena, notwithstanding the title of Prince of Eslingen (or Essling), which he had won under the walls of Vienna, was no longer "the favourite child of victory" as he had been at Zurich.

Having mentioned Massena I may observe that he did not favour the change of the French Government on the foundation of the Empire. Massena loved two things, glory and money; but as to what is termed honours, he only valued those which resulted from the command of an army; and his recollections all bound him to the Republic, because the Republic recalled to his mind the most brilliant and glorious events of his military career. He was, besides, among the number of the Marshals who wished to see a limit put to the ambition of Bonaparte; and he had assuredly done enough, since the commencement of the wars of the Republic, to be permitted to enjoy some repose, which his health at that period required. What could he achieve against the English in Portugal? The combined forces of England and Portugal daily augmented, while ours diminished. No efforts were spared by England to gain a superiority in the great struggle in which she was engaged; as her money was lavished profusely, her troops paid well wherever they went, and were abundantly supplied with ammunition and provisions: the French army was compelled, though far from possessing such ample means, to purchase at the same high rate, in order to keep the natives from joining the English party. But even this did not prevent numerous partial insurrections in different places, which rendered all communication with France extremely difficult. Armed bands continually carried off our dispersed soldiers; and the presence of the British troops, supported by the money they spent in the country, excited the inhabitants against us; for it is impossible to suppose that, unsupported by the English, Portugal could have held out a single moment against France. But battles, bad weather, and even want, had so reduced the French force that it was absolutely necessary our troops should repose when their enterprises could lead to no results. In this state of things Massena was recalled, because his health was so materially injured as to render it impossible for him to exert sufficient activity to restore the army to a respectable footing.

Under these circumstances Bonaparte sent Bertrand into Illyria to take the place of Marmont, who was ordered in his turn to relieve Massena and take command of the French army in Portugal Marmont on assuming the command found the troops in a deplorable state. The difficulty of procuring provisions was extreme, and the means he was compelled to employ for that purpose greatly heightened the evil, at the same time insubordination and want of discipline prevailed to such an alarming degree that it would be as difficult as painful to depict the situation of our army at this period, Marmont, by his steady conduct, fortunately succeeded in correcting the disorders which prevailed, and very soon found himself at the head of a well-organised army, amounting to 30,000 infantry, with forty pieces of artillery, but he had only a very small body of cavalry, and those ill-mounted.

Affairs in Spain at the commencement of 1811 exhibited an aspect not very different from those of Portugal. At first we were uniformly successful, but our advantages were so dearly purchased that the ultimate issue of this struggle might easily have been foreseen, because when a people fight for their homes and their liberties the invading army must gradually diminish, while at the same time the armed population, emboldened by success, increases in a still more marked progression. Insurrection was now regarded by the Spaniards as a holy and sacred duty, to which the recent meetings of the Cortes in the Isle of Leon had given, as it were, a legitimate character, since Spain found again, in the remembrance of her ancient privileges, at least the shadow of a Government—a centre around which the defenders of the soil of the Peninsula could rally.

```
—[Lord Wellington gave Massena a beating at Fuentes d'Onore on the
5th of May 1811.  It was soon after this battle that Napoleon sent
Marmont to succeed Massena.  Advancing on the southern frontier of
Portugal the skillful Soult contrived to take Badajoz from a
wavering Spanish garrison.  About this time, however, General
Graham, with his British corps, sallied out of Cadiz, and beat the
French on the heights of Barrosa, which lie in front of Cadiz, which
city the French were then besieging.  Encouraged by the successes of
our regular armies, the Spanish Guerillas became more and more
numerous and daring.  By the end of 1811 Joseph Bonaparte found so
many thorns in his usurped crown that he implored his brother to put
it on some other head.  Napoleon would not then listen to his
prayer.  In the course of 1811 a plan was laid for liberating
Ferdinand from his prison in France and placing him at the head of
affairs in Spain, but was detected by the emissaries of Bonaparte's
police.  Ferdinand's sister, the ex-Queen of Etruria, had also
planned an escape to England.  Her agents were betrayed, tried by a
military commission, and shot—the Princess herself was condemned to
close confinement in a Roman convent.—Editor of 1836 edition.]—
```

The Continental system was the cause, if not of the eventual fall, at least of the rapid fall of Napoleon. This cannot be doubted if we consider for a moment the brilliant situation of the Empire in 1811, and the effect simultaneously produced throughout Europe by that system, which undermined the most powerful throne which ever existed. It was the Continental system that Napoleon upheld in Spain, for he had persuaded himself that this system, rigorously enforced, would strike a death blow to the commerce of England; and Duroc besides informed me of a circumstance which is of great weight in this question. Napoleon one day said to him, "I am no longer anxious that Joseph should be King of Spain; and he himself is indifferent about it. I would give the crown to the first comer who would shut his ports against the English."

Murat had come to Paris on the occasion of the Empress' accouchement, and I saw him several times during his stay, for we had always been on the best terms; and I must do him the justice to say that he never assumed the King but to his courtiers, and those who had known him only as a monarch. Eight or ten days after the birth of the King of Rome, as I was one morning walking in the Champs Elysees, I met Murat. He was alone, and dressed in a long blue overcoat. We were exactly opposite the gardens of his sister–in–law, the Princess Borghese. "Well, Bourrienne," said Murat, after we had exchanged the usual courtesies, "well, what are you about now?" I informed him how I had been treated by Napoleon, who, that I might not be in Hamburg when the decree of union arrived there, had recalled me to Paris under a show of confidence. I think I still see the handsome and expressive countenance of Joachim when, having addressed him by the titles of Sire and Your Majesty, he said to me, "Pshaw! Bourrienne, are we not old comrades? The Emperor has treated you unjustly; and to whom has he not been unjust? His displeasure is preferable to his favour, which costs so dear! He says that he made us Kings; but did we not make him an Emperor? To you, my friend, whom I have known long and intimately, I can make my profession of faith. My sword, my blood, my life belong to the Emperor. When he calls me to the field to combat his enemies and the enemies of France I am no longer a King, I resume the rank of a Marshal of the Empire; but let him require no more. At Naples I will be King of Naples, and I will not sacrifice to his false calculations the life, the well–being, and the interests of my subjects. Let him not imagine that he can treat me as he has treated Louis! For I am ready to defend, even against him, if it must be so, the rights of the people over whom he has appointed me to rule. Am I then an advance–guard King?" These last words appeared to me peculiarly appropriate in the mouth of Murat, who had always served in the advance– guard of our armies, and I thought expressed in a very happy manner the similarity of his situation as a king and a soldier.

I walked with Murat about half an hour. In the course of our conversation he informed me that his greatest cause of complaint against the Emperor was his having first put him forward and then abandoned him. "Before I arrived in Naples," continued he, "it was intimated to me that there was a design of assassinating me. What did I do? I entered that city alone, in full daylight, in an open carriage, for I would rather have been assassinated at once than have lived in the constant fear of being so. I afterwards made a descent on the Isle of Capri, which succeeded. I attempted one against Sicily, and am curtain it would have also been successful had the Emperor fulfilled his promise of sending the Toulon fleet to second my operations; but he issued contrary orders: he enacted Mazarin, and unshed me to play the part of the adventurous Duke of Guise. But I see through his designs. Now that he has a son, on whom he has bestowed the title of King of Rome, he merely wishes the crown of Naples to be considered as a deposit in my hands. He regards Naples as a future annexation to the Kingdom of Rome, to which I foresee it is his design to unite the whole of Italy. But let him not urge me too far, for I will oppose him, and conquer, or perish in the attempt, sword in hand."

I had the discretion not to inform Murat how correctly he had divined the plans of the Emperor and his projects as to Italy, but in regard to the Continental system, which, perhaps, the reader will be inclined to call my great stalking-horse, I spoke of it as I had done to the Prince of Sweden, and I perceived that he was fully disposed to follow my advice, as experience has sufficiently proved. It was in fact the Continental system which separated the interests of Murat from those of the Emperor, and which compelled the new King of Naples to form alliances amongst the Princes at war with France. Different opinions have been entertained on this Subject; mine is, that the Marshal of the Empire was wrong, but the King of Naples right.

The Princes and Dukes of the Empire must pardon me for so often designating them by their Republican names. The Marshals set less value on their titles of nobility than the Dukes and Counts selected from among the civilians. Of all the sons of the Republic Regnault de St. Jean d'Angely was the most gratified at being a Count, whilst, among the fathers of the Revolution no one could regard with greater disdain than Fouche his title of Duke of Otranto; he congratulated himself upon its possession only once, and that was after the fall of the Empire.

I have expressed my dislike of Fouche; and the reason of that feeling was, that I could not endure his system of making the police a government within a government. He had left Paris before my return thither, but I had frequent occasion to speak of that famous personage to Savary, whom, for the reason above assigned, I do not always term Duc de Rovigo. Savary knew better than any one the fallacious measures of Fouche's administration, since he was his successor. Fouche, under pretence of encouraging men of letters, though well aware that the Emperor was hostile to them, intended only to bring them into contempt by making them write verses at command. It was easily seen that Napoleon nourished a profound dislike of literary men, though we must not conclude that he wished the public to be aware of that dislike. Those, besides, who devoted their pens to blazon his glory and his power were sure to be received by him with distinction. On the other hand, as Charlemagne and Louis XIV. owed a portion of the splendour of their reigns to the lustre reflected on them by literature, he wished to appear to patronise authors, provided that they never discussed questions relating to philosophy, the independence of mankind, and civil and political rights. With regard to men of science it was wholly different; those he held in real estimation; but men of letters, properly so called, were considered by him merely as a sprig in his Imperial crown.

The marriage of the Emperor with an Archduchess of Austria had set all the Court poets to work, and in this contest of praise and flattery it must be confessed that the false gods were vanquished by the true God; for, in spite of their fulsome verses, not one of the disciples of Apollo could exceed the extravagance of the Bishops in their pastoral letters. At a time when so many were striving to force themselves into notice there still existed a feeling of esteem in the public mind for men of superior talent who remained independent amidst the general corruption; such was M. Lemercier, such was M. de Chateaubriand. I was in Paris in the spring of 1811, at the period of Chenier's death, when the numerous friends whom Chateaubriand possessed in the second class of the Institute looked to him as the successor of Chenier. This was more than a mere literary question, not only on account of the high literary reputation M. de Chateaubriand already possessed, but of the recollection of his noble conduct at the period of Duc d'Enghien's death, which was yet fresh in the memory of every one; and, besides, no person could be ignorant of the immeasurable difference of opinion between Chenier and M. de Chateaubriand.

M. de Chateaubriand obtained a great majority of votes, and was elected a Member of the Institute. This opened a wide field for conjecture in Paris. Every one was anxious to see how the author of the Genie du Christianisme, the faithful defender of the Bourbons, would bend his eloquence to pronounce the eulogium of a regicide. The time for the admission of the new Member of the Institute arrived, but in his discourse, copies of which were circulated in Paris, he had ventured to allude to the death of Louis XVI., and to raise his voice against the regicides. This did not displease Napoleon; but M. de Chateaubriand also made a profession of faith in favour of liberty, which, he said, found refuge amongst men of letters when banished from the politic body. This was great boldness for the time; for though Bonaparte was secretly gratified at seeing the judges of Louis XVI. scourged by an heroic pen, yet those men held the highest situations under the Government. Cambaceres filled the second place in the Empire, although at a great distance from the first; Merlin de Douai was also in power; and it is known how much liberty was stifled and hidden beneath the dazzling illusion of what is termed glory. A commission was named to examine the discourse of Chateaubriand. MM. Suard, de Segur, de Fontanes, and two or three other members of the same class of the Institute whose names I cannot recollect, were of opinion that the discourse should be read; but it was opposed by the majority.

When Napoleon was informed of what had passed he demanded a sight of the address, which was presented to him by M. Daru. After having perused it he exclaimed; "Had this discourse been delivered I would have shut the gates of the Institute, and thrown M. de Chateaubriand into a dungeon for life." The storm long raged; at length means of conciliation were tried. The Emperor required M. de Chateaubriand to prepare another discourse, which the latter refused to do, in spite of every menace. Madame Gay applied to Madame Regnault de St. Jean d'Angely, who interested her husband in favour of the author of the Genie du Christianisme. M. de Montalivet and Savary also acted on this occasion in the most praiseworthy manner, and succeeded in appeasing the first transports of the Emperor's rage. But the name of Chateaubriand constantly called to mind the circumstances which had occasioned him to give in his resignation; and, besides, Napoleon had another complaint against him. He had published in the 'Merceure' an article on a work of M. Alexandre de Laborde. In that article, which was eagerly read in Paris, and which caused the suppression of the 'Merceure', occurred the famous phrase which has been since so often repeated: "In vain a Nero triumphs: Tacitus is already born in his Empire." This quotation leads me to repeat an observation, which, I believe, I have already made, viz. that it is a manifest misconception to compare Bonaparte to Nero. Napoleon's ambition might blind his vision to political crimes, but in private life no man could evince less disposition to cruelty or bloodshed. A proof that he bore little resemblance to Nero is that his anger against the author of the article in question vented itself in mere words. "What!" exclaimed he, "does Chateaubriand think I am a fool, and that I do not know what he means? If he goes on this way I will have him sabred on the steps of the Tuileries." This language is quite characteristic of Bonaparte, but it was uttered in the first ebullition of his wrath. Napoleon merely threatened, but Nero would have made good his threat; and in such a case there is surely some difference between words and deeds.

The discourse of M. de Chateaubriand revived Napoleon's former enmity against him; he received an order to quit Paris: M. Daru returned to him the manuscript of his discourse, which had been read by Bonaparte, who cancelled some passages with a pencil. We can be sure that the phrase about liberty was not one of those spared by the Imperial pencil. However that may be, written copies were circulated with text altered and abbreviated; and I have even been told that a printed edition appeared, but I have never seen any copies; and as I do not find the discourse in the works of M. de Chateaubriand I have reason to believe that the author has not yet wished to publish it.

Such were the principal circumstances attending the nomination of Chateaubriand to the Institute. I shall not relate some others which occurred on a previous occasion, viz. on the election of an old and worthy visitor at Malmaison, M. Lemercier, and which will serve to show one of those strange inconsistencies so frequent in the character of Napoleon.

After the foundation of the Empire M. Lemercier ceased to present himself at the Tuileries, St. Cloud, or at Malmaison, though he was often seen in the salons of Madame Bonaparte while she yet hoped not to become a Queen. Two places were vacant at once in the second class of the Institute, which still contained a party favourable to liberty. This party, finding it impossible to influence the nomination of both members, contented itself with naming one, it being the mutual condition, in return for favouring the Government candidate, that the Government party should not oppose the choice of the liberals. The liberal party selected M. Lemercier, but as they knew his former connection with Bonaparte had been broken off they wished first to ascertain that he would do nothing to commit their choice. Chenier was empowered to inquire whether M. Lemercier would refuse to accompany them to the Tuileries when they repaired thither in a body, and whether, on his election, he would comply with the usual ceremony of being presented to the Emperor. M. Lemercier replied that he would do nothing contrary to the customs and usages of the body to which he might belong: he was accordingly elected. The Government candidate was M. Esmenard, who was also elected. The two new members were presented to the Emperor on the same day. On this occasion upwards of 400 persons were present in the salon, from one of whom I received these details. When the Emperor saw M. Lemercier, for whom he had long pretended great friendship, he said to him in a kind tone, "Well, Lemercier, you are now installed." Lemercier respectfully bowed to the Emperor; but without uttering a word of reply. Napoleon was mortified at this silence, but without saying anything more to Lemercier he turned to Esmenard, the member who should have been most acceptable to him, and vented upon him the whole weight of his indignation in a manner equally unfeeling and unjust. "Well, Esmenard," said he, "do you still hold your place in the police?" These words were spoken in so loud a tone as to be heard by all present; and it was doubtless this cruel and ambiguous speech which furnished the enemies of Esmenard with arms to attack his reputation as a man of honour, and to give an appearance of disgrace to those functions which he exercised with so much zeal and ability.

The Memoirs of Napoleon, V11, 1812

When, at the commencement of 1811, I left Paris I had ceased to delude myself respecting the brilliant career which seemed opening before me during the Consulate. I clearly perceived that since Bonaparte, instead of receiving me as I expected, had refused to see me at all, the calumnies of my enemies were triumphant, and that I had nothing to hope for from an absolute ruler, whose past injustice rendered him the more unjust. He now possessed what he had so long and ardently wished for, —a son of his own, an inheritor of his name, his power, and his throne. I must take this opportunity of stating that the malevolent and infamous rumours spread abroad respecting the birth of the King of Rome were wholly without foundation. My friend Corvisart, who did not for a single instant leave Maria Louisa during her long and painful labour, removed from my mind every doubt on the subject. It is as true that the young Prince, for whom the Emperor of Austria stood sponsor at the font, was the son of Napoleon and the Archduchess Maria Louisa as it is false that Bonaparte was the father of the first child of Hortense. The birth of the son of Napoleon was hailed with general enthusiasm. The Emperor was at the height of his power from the period of the birth of his son until the reverse he experienced after the battle of the Moskowa. The Empire, including the States possessed by the Imperial family, contained nearly 57,000,000 of inhabitants; but the period was fast approaching when this power, unparalleled in modern times, was to collapse under its own weight.

—[The little King of Rome, Napoleon Francis Bonaparte, was born on the 20th of March 1811. Editor of 1836 edition.]—

CHAPTER XXVI.

My return to Hamburg—Government Committee established there—
Anecdote of the Comte de Chaban—Napoleon's misunderstanding with
the Pope—Cardinal Fesch—Convention of a Council Declaration
required from the Bishops—Spain in 1811—Certainty of war with
Russia—Lauriston supersedes Caulaincourt at St. Petersburg—The war
in Spain neglected—Troops of all nations at the disposal of
Bonaparte—Levy of the National Guard—Treaties with Prussia and
Austria—Capitulation renewed with Switzerland—Intrigues with
Czernischeff—Attacks of my enemies—Memorial to the Emperor—Ogier
de la Saussaye and the mysterious box—Removal of the Pope to
Fontainebleau—Anecdote of His Holiness and M. Denon—Departure of
Napoleon and Maria Louisa for Dresden—Situation of affairs in Spain
and Portugal—Rapp's account of the Emperor's journey to Dantzic—

The Memoirs of Napoleon, V11, 1812

```
Mutual wish for war on the part of Napoleon and Alexander—Sweden
and Turkey—Napoleon's vain attempt to detach Sweden from her
alliance with Russia.
```

As I took the most lively interest in all that concerned the Hanse Towns, my first care on returning to Hamburg was to collect information from the most respectable sources concerning the influential members of the new Government. Davoust was at its head. On his arrival he had established in the Duchy of Mecklenburg, in Swedish Pomerania, and in Stralsund, the capital of that province, military posts and custom-houses, and that in a time of profound peace with those countries, and without any previous declaration. The omnipotence of Napoleon, and the terror inspired by the name of Davoust, overcame all obstacles which might have opposed those iniquitous usurpations. The weak were forced to yield to the strong.

At Hamburg a Government Committee was formed, consisting of the Prince of Eckmuhl as President, Comte de Chaban, Councillor of State, who superintended the departments of the Interior and Finance, and of M. Faure, Councillor of State, who was appointed to form and regulate the Courts of Law. I had sometimes met M. de Chaban at Malmaison. He was distantly related to Josephine, and had formerly been an officer in the French Guards. He was compelled to emigrate, having been subjected to every species of persecution during the Revolution.

M. de Chaban was among the first of the emigrants who returned to France after the 18th Brumaire. He was at first made Sub-Prefect of Vendome, but on the union of Tuscany with France Napoleon created him a member of the Junta appointed to regulate the affairs of Tuscany. He next became Prefect of Coblentz and Brussels, was made a Count by Bonaparte, and was afterwards chosen a member of the Government Committee at Hamburg. M. de Chaban was a man of upright principles, and he discharged his various functions in a way that commanded esteem and attachment.

```
—[I recollect an anecdote which but too well depicts those
disastrous times.  The Comte de Chaban, being obliged to cross
France during the Reign of Terror, was compelled to assume a,
disguise.  He accordingly provided himself with a smockfrock; a cart
and horses, and a load of corn.  In this manner he journeyed from
place to place till he reached the frontiers.  He stopped at
Rochambeau, in the Vendomais, where he was recognised by the Marshal
de Rochambeau, who to guard against exciting any suspicion among-
```

The Memoirs of Napoleon, V11, 1812

```
his servants, treated him as if he had really been a carman and said
to him, "You may dine in the kitchen."—Bourrienne.]—
```

The Hanseatic Towns, united to the Grand Empire professedly for their welfare, soon felt the blessings of the new organisation of a regenerating Government. They were at once presented with; the stamp– duty, registration, the lottery, the droits reunis, the tax on cards, and the 'octroi'. This prodigality of presents caused, as we may be sure, the most lively gratitude; a tax for military quarters and for warlike supplies was imposed, but this did not relieve any one from laving not only officers and soldiers; but even all the chiefs of the administration and their officials billeted on them: The refineries, breweries, and manufactures of all sorts were suppressed. The cash chests of the Admiralty, of the charity houses, of the manufactures, of the savings– banks, of the working classes, the funds of the prisons, the relief meant for the infirm, the chests of the refuges, orphanages; and of the hospitals, were all seized.

More than 200,000 men, Italian, Dutch, and French soldiers came in turn to stay there, but only to be clothed and shod; and then they left newly clothed from head to foot. To leave nothing to be wished for, Davoust, from 1812, established military commissions in all the thirty-second. military division, before he entered upon the Russian campaign. To complete these oppressive measures he established at the same time the High Prevotal Court of the Customs. It was at this time that M. Eudes, the director of the ordinary customs, a strict but just man, said that the rule of the ordinary customs would be regretted, "for till now you have only been on roses.." The professed judgments of this court were executed without appeal and without delay. From what I have just said the situation and the misery of the north of Germany, and the consequent discontent, can be judged.

During my stay in Hamburg, which on this occasion was not very long, Napoleon's attention was particularly engaged by the campaign of Portugal, and his discussions with the Pope. At this period the thunderbolts of Rome were not very alarming. Yet precautions were taken to keep secret the excommunication which Pius VII. had pronounced against Napoleon. The event, however, got reported about, and a party in favour of the Pope speedily rose up among the clergy, and more particularly among the fanatics. Napoleon sent to Savona the Archbishops of Nantes, Bourges, Treves, and Tours, to endeavour to bring about a reconciliation with His Holiness. But all their endeavours were unavailing, and after staying a month at Savona they returned to Paris without having done anything. But Napoleon was not discouraged by this first disappointment, and he shortly afterwards sent a second deputation, which experienced the same fate as the first. Cardinal Fesch, Napoleon's uncle, took part with the Pope. For this fact I can vouch, though I cannot for an answer which he is said to have made to the Emperor. I have been informed that when Napoleon was one day speaking to his uncle about the Pope's obstinacy the Cardinal made some observations to him on his (Bonaparte's) conduct to the Holy Father, upon which Napoleon flew into a passion, and said that the Pope and he were two old fools. "As for the Pope," said he, "he is too obstinate to listen to anything. No, I am determined he shall never have Rome again . . . . He will not remain at Savona, and where does he wish I should send him?"—"To Heaven, perhaps," replied the Cardinal.

The truth is, the Emperor was violently irritated against Pius VII. Observing with uneasiness the differences and difficulties to which all these dissensions gave rise, he was anxious to put a stop to them. As the Pope would not listen to any propositions that were made to him, Napoleon convoked a Council, which assembled in Paris, and at which several Italian Bishops were present. The Pope insisted that the temporal and spiritual interests should be discussed together; and, however disposed a certain number of prelates, particularly the Italians, might be to separate these two points of discussion, yet the influence of the Church and well-contrived intrigues gradually gave preponderance to the wishes of the Pope. The Emperor, having discovered that a secret correspondence was carried on by several of the Bishops and Archbishops who had seats in the Council, determined to get rid of some of them, and the Bishops of Ghent, Troyes, Tournay, and Toulouse were arrested and sent to Vincennes. They were superseded by others. He wished to dissolve the Council, which he saw was making no advance towards the object he had in view, and, fearing that it might adopt some act at variance with his supreme wish, every member of the Council was individually required to make a declaration that the proposed changes were conformable to the laws of the Church. It was said at the time that they were unanimous in this individual declaration, though it is certain that in the sittings of the Council opinions were divided. I know not what His Holiness thought of these written opinions compared with the verbal opinions that had been delivered, but certain it is though still a captive at Savona, he refused to adhere to the concessions granted in the secret declarations.

The conflicts which took place in Spain during the year 1811 were unattended by any decisive results. Some brilliant events, indeed, attested the courage of our troops and the skill of our generals. Such were the battle of Albufera and the taking of Tarragona, while Wellington was obliged to raise the siege of Badajoz. These advantages, which were attended only by glory, encouraged Napoleon in the hope of triumphing in the Peninsula, and enabled him to enjoy the brilliant fetes which took place at Paris in celebration of the birth of the King of Rome.

On his return from a tour in Holland at the end of October Napoleon clearly saw that a rupture with Russia was inevitable. In vain he sent Lauriston as Ambassador to St. Petersburg to supersede Caulaincourt, who would no longer remain there: all the diplomatic skill in the world could effect nothing with a powerful Government which had already formed its determination. All the Cabinets in Europe were now unanimous in wishing for the overthrow of Napoleon's power, and the people no less, ardently wished for an order of things less fatal to their trade and industry. In the state to which Europe was reduced no one could counteract the wish of Russia and her allies to go to war with France—Lauriston no more than Caulaincourt.

The war for which Napoleon was now obliged to prepare forced him to neglect Spain, and to leave his interests in that country in a state of real danger. Indeed, his occupation of Spain and his well-known wish to maintain himself there were additional motives for inducing the powers of Europe to enter upon a war which would necessarily divide Napoleon's forces. All at once the troops which were in Italy and the north of Germany moved towards the frontiers of the Russian Empire. From March 1811 the Emperor had all the military forces of Europe at his disposal. It was curious to see this union of nations, distinguished by difference of manners,

```
[It should be remarked that Napoleon was far from being anxious
for the war with Russia. Metternich writing on 26th March 1811,
says "Everything seems to indicate that the Emperor Napoleon is at
present still far from desiring a war with Russia. But it is not
less true that the Emperor Alexander has given himself over, 'nolens
volens', to the war party, and that he will bring about war, because
the time is approaching when he will no longer be able to resist the
reaction of the party in the internal affairs of his Empire, or the
temper of his army. The contest between Count Romanzov and the
party opposed to that Minister seems on the point of precipitating a
war between Russia and France." This, from Metternich, is strong
evidence.]–
```

language, religion, and interests, all ready to fight for one man against a power who had done nothing to offend them. Prussia herself, though she could not pardon the injuries he had inflicted upon her, joined his alliance, but with the intention of breaking it on the first opportunity. When the war with Russia was first spoken of Savary and I had frequent conversations on the subject. I communicated to him all the intelligence I received from abroad respecting that vast enterprise. The Duc de Rovigo shared all my forebodings; and if he and those who thought like him had been listened to, the war would probably have been avoided. Through him I learnt who were the individuals who urged the invasion. The eager ambition with which they looked forward to Viceroyalties, Duchies, and endowments blinded them to the possibility of seeing the Cossacks in Paris.

The gigantic enterprise being determined on, vast preparations were made for carrying it into effect. Before his departure Napoleon, who was to take with him all the disposable troops, caused a 'Senatus–consulte' to be issued for levying the National Guards, who were divided into three corps. He also arranged his diplomatic affairs by concluding, in February 1812, a treaty of alliance, offensive and defensive, with Prussia, by virtue of which the two contracting powers mutually guaranteed the integrity of their own possessions, and the European possessions of the Ottoman Porte, because that power was then at war with Russia. A similar treaty was concluded about the beginning of March with Austria, and about the end of the same month Napoleon renewed the capitulation of France and Switzerland. At length, in the month of April, there came to light an evident proof of the success which had attended M. Czernischeff's intrigues in Paris. It was ascertained that a clerk in the War Office, named Michel, had communicated to him the situation of the French forces in Germany. Michel was condemned to death, for the time was gone by when Bonaparte, confident in his genius and good fortune, could communicate his plans to the spy of General Melas.

In March 1812, when I saw that the approaching war would necessarily take Napoleon from France, weary of the persecutions and even threats by which I was every day assailed, I addressed to the Emperor a memorial explaining my conduct and showing the folly and wickedness of my accusers. Among them was a certain Ogier de la Saussaye, who had sent a report to the Emperor, in which the principal charge was, that I had carried off a box containing important papers belonging to the First Consul. The accusation of Ogier de la Saussaye terminated thus: "I add to my report the interrogatories of MM. Westphalen, Osy, Chapeau Rouge, Aukscher, Thierry, and Gumprecht–Mores. The evidence of the latter bears principally on a certain mysterious box, a secret upon which it is impossible to throw any light, but the reality of which we are bound to believe." These are his words. The affair of the mysterious box has been already explained. I have already informed the reader that I put my papers into a box, which I buried lest it should be stolen from me. But for that precaution I should not have been able to lay before the reader the autograph documents in my possession, and which I imagine form the most essential part of these volumes. In my memorial to the Emperor I said, in allusion to the passage above quoted, "This, Sire, is the most atrocious part of Ogier's report.

"Gumprecht being questioned on this point replies that the accuser has probably, as well as himself, seen the circumstance mentioned in an infamous pamphlet which appeared seven or eight years, ago. It was, I think, entitled 'Le Secret du Cabinet des Tuileries,' and was very likely at the time of its appearance denounced by the police. In that libel it is stated, among a thousand other calumnies equally false and absurd, 'that when I left the First Consul I carried away a box full of important papers, that I was in consequence sent to the Temple, where your brother Joseph came to me and offered me my liberation, and a million of francs, if I would restore the papers, which I refused to do,' etc. Ogier, instead of looking for this libel in Hamburg, where I read it, has the impudence to give credit to the charge, the truth of which could have been ascertained immediately: and he adds, 'This secret we are bound to believe.' Your Majesty knows whether I was ever in the Temple, and whether Joseph ever made such an offer to me." I entreated that the Emperor would do me the favour to bring me to trial; for certainly I should have regarded that as a favour rather than to remain as I was, exposed to vague accusations; yet all my solicitations were in vain. My letter to the Emperor remained unanswered; but though Bonaparte could not spare a few moments to reply to an old friend, I learned through Duroc the contempt he cherished for my accusers. Duroc advised me not to be uneasy, and that in all probability the Emperor's prejudices against me would be speedily overcome; and I must say that if they were not overcome it was neither the fault of Duroc nor Savary, who knew how to rightly estimate the miserable intrigues just alluded to.

Napoleon was at length determined to extend the limits of his Empire, or rather to avenge the injuries which Russia had committed against his Continental system. Yet, before he departed for Germany, the resolute refusal of the Pope to submit to any arrangement urgently claimed his consideration. Savona did not appear to him a sufficiently secure residence for such a prisoner. He feared that when all his strength should be removed towards the Niemen the English might carry off the Pope, or that the Italians, excited by the clergy, whose dissatisfaction was general in Italy, would stir up those religious dissensions which are always fatal and difficult to quell. With the view, therefore, of keeping the Pope under his control he removed him to Fontainebleau, and even at one time thought of bringing him to Paris.

The Emperor appointed M. Denon to reside with the Pope at Fontainebleau; and to afford his illustrious prisoner the society of such a man was certainly a delicate mark of attention on the part of Napoleon. When speaking of his residence with Pius VII. M. Denon related to me the following anecdote. "The Pope," said he, "was much attached to me. He always addressed me by the appellation 'my son,' and he loved to converse with me, especially on the subject of the Egyptian expedition. One day he asked me for my work on Egypt, which he said he wished to read; and as you know it is not quite orthodox, and does not perfectly agree with the creation of the world according to Genesis, I at first hesitated; but the Pope insisted, and at length I complied with his wish. The Holy Father assured me that he had been much interested by the perusal of the book. I made some allusion to the delicate points; upon which he said, "No matter, no matter, my son; all that is exceedingly curious, and I must confess entirely new to me." I then," continued M. Denon, told His Holiness why I hesitated to lend him the work, which, I observed, he had excommunicated, together with its author. "Excommunicated you, my son?" resumed the Pope in a tone of affectionate concern. "I am very sorry for it, and assure you I was far from being aware of any such thing."

When M. Denon related to me this anecdote he told me how greatly he had admired the virtues and resignation of the Holy Father; but he added that it would nevertheless have been easier to make him a martyr than to induce him to yield on any point until he should be restored to the temporal sovereignty of Rome, of which he considered himself the depositary, and which he would not endure the reproach of having willingly sacrificed. After settling the place of the Pope's residence Napoleon set off for Dresden, accompanied by Maria Louisa, who had expressed a wish to see her father.

The Russian enterprise, the most gigantic, perhaps, that the genius of man ever conceived since the conquest of India by Alexander, now absorbed universal attention, and defied the calculations of reason. The Manzanares was forgotten, and nothing was thought of but the Niemen, already so celebrated by the raft of Tilsit. Thither, as towards a common centre, were moving men, horses, provisions, and baggage of every kind, from all parts of Europe. The hopes of our generals and the fears of all prudent men were directed to

The Memoirs of Napoleon, V11, 1812

Russia. The war in Spain, which was becoming more and more unfortunate, excited but a feeble interest; and our most distinguished officers looked upon it as a disgrace to be sent to the Peninsula. In short, it was easy to foresee that the period was not far distant when the French would be obliged to recross the Pyrenees. Though the truth was concealed from the Emperor on many subjects, yet he was not deceived as to the situation of Spain in the spring of 1812. In February the Duke of Ragusa had frankly informed him that the armies of Spain and Portugal could not, without considerable reinforcements of men and money, hope for any important advantages since Ciudad-Rodrigo and Badajoz had fallen into the hands of the English.

Before he commenced his great operations on the Niemen and the Volga Napoleon made a journey to Dantzic, and Rapp, who was then Governor of that city, informed me of some curious particulars connected with the Imperial visit. The fact is, that if Rapp's advice had been listened to, and had been supported by men higher in rank than himself, Bonaparte would not have braved the chances of the Russian war until those chances turned against him. Speaking to me of the Russians Rapp said, "They will soon be as wise as we are! Every time we go to war with them we teach them how to beat us." I was struck with the originality and truth of this observation, which at the time I heard it was new, though it has been often repeated since.

"On leaving Dresden," said Rapp to me, "Napoleon came to Dantzic. I expected a dressing; for, to tell you the truth, I had treated very cavalierly both his custom-house and its officers, who were raising up as many enemies to France as there were inhabitants in my Government. I had also warned him of all that has since happened in Russia, but I assure you I did not think myself quite so good a prophet. In the beginning of 1812 I thus wrote to him: 'If your Majesty should experience reverses you may depend on it that both Russians and Germans will rise up in a mass to shake off the yoke. There will be a crusade, and all your allies will abandon you. Even the King of Bavaria, on whom you rely so confidently, will join the coalition. I except only the King of Saxony. He, perhaps, might remain faithful to you; but his subjects will force him to make common cause with your enemies. The King of Naples," continued Rapp, "who had the command of the cavalry, had been to Dantzic before the Emperor. He did not seem to take a more favourable view of the approaching campaign than I did. Murat was dissatisfied that the Emperor would not consent to his rejoining him in Dresden; and he said that he would rather be a captain of grenadiers than a King such as he was."

The Memoirs of Napoleon, V11, 1812

Here I interrupted Rapp to tell him what had fallen from Murat when I met him in the Champs Elysees "Bah!" resumed Rapp, "Murat, brave as he was, was a craven in Napoleon's presence! On the Emperor's arrival in Dantzic the first thing of which he spoke to me was the alliance he had just then concluded with Prussia and Austria. I could not refrain from telling him that we did a great deal of mischief as allies; a fact of which I was assured from the reports daily transmitted to me respecting the conduct of our troops. Bonaparte tossed his bead, as you know he was in the habit of doing when he was displeased. After a moment's silence, dropping the familiar thee and thou, he said, 'Monsieur le General, this is a torrent which must be allowed to run itself out. It will not last long. I must first ascertain whether Alexander decidedly wishes for war.' Then, suddenly changing the subject of conversation, he said, `Have you not lately observed something extraordinary in Murat? I think he is quite altered. Is be ill?'—`Sire,' replied I, 'Murat is not ill, but he is out of spirits.'—`Out of spirits! but why? Is he not satisfied with being a King?'—`Sire, Murat says he is no King.'—`That is his own fault. Why does he make himself a Neapolitan? Why is he not a Frenchman? When he is in his Kingdom he commits all sorts of follies. He favours the trade of England; that I will not suffer.'

"When," continued Rapp, "he spoke of the favour extended by Murat to the trade between Naples and England I thought my turn would come next; but I was deceived. No more was said on the subject, and when I was about to take my leave the Emperor said to me, as when in his best of humours, 'Rapp, you will sup with me this evening.' I accordingly supped that evening with the Emperor, who had also invited the King of Naples and Berthier. Next day the Emperor visited the fortress, and afterwards returned to the Government Palace, where he received the civil and military authorities. He again invited Murat, Berthier, and me to supper. When we first sat down to table we were all very dull, for the Emperor was silent; and, as you well know, under such circumstances not even Murat himself dared to be the first to speak to him. At length Napoleon, addressing me, inquired how far it was from Cadiz to Dantzic. 'Too far, Sire,' replied I. 'I understand you, Monsieur le General, but in a few months the distance will be still greater.'—'So much the worse, Sire!' Here there was another pause. Neither Murat nor Berthier, on whom the Emperor fixed a scrutinising glance, uttered a word, and Napoleon again broke silence, but without addressing any one of us in particular: 'Gentlemen,' said be in a solemn and rather low tone of voice, 'I see plainly that you are none of you inclined to fight again. The King of Naples does not wish to leave the fine climate of his dominions, Berthier wishes to enjoy the diversion of the chase at his estate of Gros Bois, and Rapp is impatient to be back to his hotel in Paris.' Would you believe it," pursued Rapp, "that neither Murat nor Berthier said a word in reply? and the ball again came to me. I told him frankly that what he said was perfectly true, and the King of Naples and the Prince of Neufchatel complimented me on my spirit, and observed that I was quite right in saying what I did. 'Well,' said I, "since it was so very right, why did you not follow my example, and why leave me to say all?' You cannot conceive," added Rapp, "how confounded they both were, and especially Murat, though be was very differently situated from Berthier."

The negotiations which Bonaparte opened with Alexander, when he yet wished to seem averse to war, resembled those oratorical paraphrases which do not prevent us from coming to the conclusion we wish. The two Emperors equally desired war; the one with the view of consolidating his power, and the other in the hope of freeing himself from a yoke which threatened to reduce him to a state of vassalage, for it was little short of this to require a power like Russia to close her ports against England for the mere purpose of favouring the interests of France. At that time only two European powers were not tied to Napoleon's fate—Sweden and Turkey. Napoleon was anxious to gain the alliance of these two powers. With respect to Sweden his efforts were vain; and though, in fact, Turkey was then at war with Russia, yet the Grand Seignior was not now, as at the time of Sebastiani's embassy, subject to the influence of France.

The peace, which was soon concluded at Bucharest, between Russia, and Turkey increased Napoleon's embarrassment. The left of the Russian army, secured by the neutrality of Turkey, was reinforced by Bagration's corps from Moldavia: it subsequently occupied the right of the Beresina, and destroyed the last hope of saving the wreck of the French army. It is difficult to conceive how Turkey could have allowed the consideration of injuries she had received from France to induce her to terminate the war with Russia when France was attacking that power with immense forces. The Turks never had a fairer opportunity for taking revenge on Russia, and, unfortunately for Napoleon, they suffered it to escape.

Napoleon was not more successful when he sought the alliance of a Prince whose fortune he had made, and who was allied to his family, but with whom he had never been on terms of good understanding. The Emperor Alexander had a considerable corps of troops in Finland destined to protect that country against the Sweden, Napoleon having consented to that occupation in order to gain the provisional consent of Alexander to the invasion of Spain. What was the course pursued by Napoleon when, being at war with Russia, he wished to detach Sweden from her alliance with Alexander? He intimated to

The Memoirs of Napoleon, V11, 1812

Bernadotte that he had a sure opportunity of retaking Finland, a conquest which would gratify his subjects and win their attachment to him. By this alliance Napoleon wished to force Alexander not to withdraw the troops who were in the north of his Empire, but rather to augment their numbers in order to cover Finland and St. Petersburg. It was thus that Napoleon endeavoured to draw the Prince Royal into his coalition. It was of little consequence to Napoleon whether Bernadotte succeeded or not. The Emperor Alexander would nevertheless have been obliged to increase his force in Finland; that was all that Napoleon wished. In the gigantic struggle upon which France and Russia were about to enter the most trivial alliance was not to be neglected. In January 1812 Davoust invaded Swedish Pomerania without any declaration of war, and without any apparent motive. Was this inconceivable violation of territory likely to dispose the Prince Royal of Sweden to the proposed alliance, even had that alliance not been adverse to the interests of his country? That was impossible; and Bernadotte took the part which was expected of him. He rejected the offers of Napoleon, and prepared for coming events.

The Emperor Alexander wished to withdraw his force from Finland for the purpose of more effectively opposing the immense army which threatened his States. Unwilling to expose Finland to an attack on the part of Sweden, he had an interview on the 28th of August 1812, at Abo, with the Prince-Royal, to come to an arrangement with him for uniting their interests. I know that the Emperor of Russia pledged himself, whatever might happen, to protect Bernadotte against the fate of the new dynasties, to guarantee the possession of his throne, and promised that he should have Norway as a compensation for Finland. He even went so far as to hint that Bernadotte might supersede Napoleon. Bernadotte adopted all the propositions of Alexander, and from that moment Sweden made common cause against Napoleon. The Prince Royal's conduct has been much blamed, but the question resolved itself into one of mere political interest. Could Bernadotte, a Swede by adoption, prefer the alliance of an ambitious sovereign whose vengeance he had to fear, and who had sanctioned the seizure of Finland to that of a powerful monarch, his formidable neighbour, his protector in Sweden, and where hostility might effectually support the hereditary claims of young Gustavus? Sweden, in joining France, would thereby have declared herself the enemy of England. Where, then, would have been her navy, her trade and even her existence?

The Memoirs of Napoleon, V11, 1812

CHAPTER XXVII. 1812.

```
Changeableness of Bonaparte's plans and opinions—Articles for the
'Moniteur' dictated by the First Consul—The Protocol of the
Congress of Chatillon—Conversations with Davoust at Hamburg—
Promise of the Viceroyalty of Poland—Hope and disappointment of the
Poles—Influence of illusion on Bonaparte—The French in Moscow—
Disasters of the retreat—Mallet's conspiracy—Intelligence of the
affair communicated to Napoleon at Smolensko—Circumstances detailed
by Rapp—Real motives of Napoleon's return to Paris—Murat, Ney, and
Eugene—Power of the Italians to endure cold—Napoleon's exertions
to repair his losses—Defection of General York—Convocation of a
Privy Council—War resolved on—Wavering of the Pope—Useless
negotiations with Vienna—Maria Louisa appointed Regent.
```

It may now he asked whether Bonaparte, previous to entering upon the last campaign, had resolved on restoring Poland to independence. The fact is that Bonaparte, as Emperor, never entertained any positive wish to reestablish the old Kingdom of Poland, though at a previous period he was strongly inclined to that re-establishment, of which he felt the necessity. He may have said that he would re-establish the Kingdom of Poland, but I beg leave to say that that is no reason for believing that he entertained any such design. He had said, and even sworn, that he would never aggrandise the territory of the Empire! The changeableness of Bonaparte's ideas, plans, and projects renders it difficult to master them; but they may be best understood when it is considered that all Napoleon's plans and conceptions varied with his fortunes. Thus, it is not unlikely that he might at one time have considered the reestablishment of Poland as essential to European policy, and afterwards have regarded it as adverse to the development of his ambition. Who can venture to guess what passed in his mind when dazzled by his glory at Dresden, and whether in one of his dreams he might not have regarded the Empire of the Jagellons as another gem in the Imperial diadem? The truth is that Bonaparte, when General-in-Chief of the army of Egypt and First Consul, had deeply at heart the avenging the dismemberment of Poland, and I have often conversed with him on this most interesting subject, upon which we entirely concurred in opinion. But times and circumstances were changed since we walked together on the terrace of Cairo and mutually deplored the death of young Sulkowski. Had Sulkowski lived Napoleon's favourable intentions with respect to Poland might perhaps have been confirmed. A fact which explains to me the coolness, I may almost say the indifference, of Bonaparte to the resurrection of Poland is that the commencement of the Consulate was the period at which that measure particularly occupied his attention. How often did he converse on the subject with me and other persons who may yet recollect his sentiments! It was the topic on which he most loved to converse, and on which he spoke with feeling and enthusiasm. In the 'Moniteur' of the period here alluded to I could point out more than one article without signature or official character which Napoleon dictated to me, and the insertion of which in that journal, considering the energy of certain expressions, sufficiently proves that they could have emanated from none but Bonaparte. It was usually in the evening that he dictated to me these articles. Then, when the affairs of the day were over, he would launch into the future, and give free scope to his vast projects. Some of these articles were characterised by so little moderation that the First Consul would very often destroy them in the morning, smiling at the violent ebullitions of the preceding night. At other times I took the liberty of not sending them to the 'Moniteur' on the night on which they were dictated, and though he might earnestly wish their insertion I adduced reasons good or bad, to account for the delay. He would then read over the article in question, and approve of my conduct; but he would sometimes add, "It is nevertheless true that with an independent Kingdom of Poland, and 150,000 disposable troops in the east of France, I should always be master of Russia, Prussia, and Austria."—"General," I would reply," I am entirely of your opinion; but wherefore awaken the suspicions of the interested parties. Leave all to time and circumstances."

The reader may have to learn, and not, perhaps, without some surprise, that in the protocol of the sittings of the Congress of Chatillon Napoleon put forward the spoliation of Poland by the three principal powers allied against him as a claim to a more advantageous peace, and to territorial indemnities for France. In policy he was right, but the report of foreign cannon was already loud enough to drown the best of arguments.

After the ill-timed and useless union of the Hanse Towns to France I returned to Hamburg in the spring of 1811 to convey my family to France. I then had some conversation with Davoust. On one occasion I said to him that if his hopes were realised, and my sad predictions respecting the war with Russia overthrown, I hoped to see the restoration of the Kingdom of Poland. Davoust replied that that event was probable, since he had Napoleon's promise of the Viceroyalty of that Kingdom, and as several of his comrades had been promised starosties. Davoust made no secret of this, and it was generally known throughout Hamburg and the north of Germany.

The Memoirs of Napoleon, V11, 1812

But notwithstanding what Davoust said respecting. Napoleon's intentions I considered that these promises had been conditional rather than positive.

On Napoleon's arrival in Poland the Diet of Warsaw, assured, as there seemed reason to be, of the Emperor's sentiments, declared the Kingdom free and independent. The different treaties of dismemberment were pronounced to be null; and certainly the Diet had a right so to act, for it calculated upon his support. But the address of the Diet to Napoleon, in which these principles were declared, was ill received. His answer was full of doubt and indecision, the motive of which could not be blamed. To secure the alliance of Austria against Russia he had just guaranteed to his father-in-law the integrity of his dominions. Napoleon therefore declared that he could take no part in any movement or resolution which might disturb Austria in the possession of the Polish provinces forming a part of her Empire. To act otherwise, he said, would be to separate himself from his alliance with Austria, and to throw her into the arms of Russia. But with regard to the Polish-Russian provinces, Napoleon declared he would see what he could do, should Providence favour the good cause. These vague and obscure expressions did not define what he intended to do for the Poles in the event of success crowning his vast enterprises. They excited the distrust of the Poles, and had no other result. On this subject, however, an observation occurs which is of some force as an apology for Napoleon. Poland was successively divided between three powers, Russia, Austria, and Prussia, with each of which Napoleon had been at war, but never with all three at once. He had therefore never been able to take advantage of his victories to re-establish Poland without injuring the interests of neutral powers or of his allies. Hence it may be concluded not only that he never had the positive will which would have triumphed over all obstacles, but also that there never was a possibility of realising those dreams and projects of revenge in which he had indulged on the banks of the Nile, as it were to console the departed spirit of Sulkowski.

Bonaparte's character presents many unaccountable incongruities. Although the most positive man that perhaps ever existed, yet there never was one who more readily yielded to the charm of illusion. In many circumstances the wish and the reality were to him one and the same thing. He never indulged in greater illusions than at the beginning of the campaign of Moscow. Even before the approach of the disasters which accompanied the most fatal retreat recorded in history, all sensible persons concurred in the opinion that the Emperor ought to have passed the winter of 1812-13 in Poland, and have resumed his vast enterprises in the spring. But his natural impatience impelled him forward as it were unconsciously, and he seemed to be under the influence of an invisible demon stronger than even his own strong will. This demon was ambition. He who knew so well the value of time, never sufficiently understood its power, and how much is sometimes gained by delay. Yet Caesar's Commentaries, which were his favourite study, ought to have shown him that Caesar did not conquer Gaul in one campaign. Another illusion by which Napoleon was misled during the campaign of Moscow, and perhaps past experience rendered it very excusable, was the belief that the Emperor Alexander would propose peace when he saw him at the head of his army on the Russian territory. The prolonged stay of Bonaparte at Moscow can indeed be accounted for in no other way than by supposing that he expected the Russian Cabinet would change its opinion and consent to treat for peace. However, whatever might have been the reason, after his long and useless stay in Moscow Napoleon left that city with the design of taking up his winter quarters in Poland; but Fate now frowned upon Napoleon, and in that dreadful retreat the elements seemed leagued with the Russians to destroy the most formidable army ever commanded by one chief. To find a catastrophe in history comparable to that of the Beresina we must go back to the destruction of the legions of Varus.

Notwithstanding the general dismay which prevailed in Paris that capital continued tranquil, when by a singular chance, on the very day on which Napoleon evacuated the burning city of Moscow, Mallet attempted his extraordinary enterprise. This General, who had always professed Republican principles, and was a man of bold decided character, after having been imprisoned for some time, obtained the permission of Government to live in Paris in a hospital house situated near the Barriere de Trove. Of Mallet's, conspiracy it is not necessary to say much after the excellent account given of it in the Memoirs of the Due de Rovigo. Mallet's plan was to make it be believed that Bonaparte had been killed at Moscow, and that a new Government was established under the authority of the Senate. But what could Mallet do? Absolutely nothing: and had his Government continued three days he would have experienced a more favourable chance than that which he ought reasonably to have expected than asserted that the Emperor was dead, but an estafette from Russia would reveal the truth, resuscitate Napoleon, and overwhelm with confusion Mallet and his proclamation. His enterprise was that of a madman. The French were too weary of troubles to throw themselves into the arms of, Mallet or his associate Lahorie, who had figured so disgracefully on the trial of Moreau., Yet, in spite of the evident impossibility of success, it must be confessed that considerable ingenuity and address marked the commencement of the conspiracy. On the 22d of October Mallet escaped from the hospital house and went to Colonel Soulier, who

The Memoirs of Napoleon, V11, 1812

commanded the tenth cohort of the National Guard, whose barracks were situated exactly behind the hospital house. Mallet was loaded with a parcel of forged orders which he had himself prepared. He introduced himself to Soulier under the name of General La Motte, and said that he came from General Mallet.

Colonel Soulier on hearing of the Emperor's death was affected to tears. He immediately ordered the adjutant to assemble the cohort and obey the orders of General La Motte, to whom he expressed his regret for being himself too ill to leave his bed. It was then two o'clock in the morning, and the forged documents respecting the Emperor's death slid the new form of Government were read to the troops by lamplight. Mallet then hastily set off with 1200 men to La Force, and liberated the Sieurs Gudal and Laholze, who were confined there. Mallet informed them of the Emperor's death and of the change of Government; gave them some orders, in obedience to which the Minister and Prefect of Police were arrested in their hotel.

I was then at Courbevoie, and I went to Paris on that very morning to breakfast, as I frequently did, with the Minister of Police. My surprise may be imagined when

```
—[General Mallet gave out that the Emperor was killed under the
walls of Moscow on the 8th of October; be could not take any other
day without incurring the risk of being contradicted by the arrival
of the regular courier.  The Emperor being dead, he concluded that
the Senate ought to be invested with the supreme authority, and he
therefore resolved to address himself in the name of that body to
the nation and the army.  In a proclamation to the soldiers he
deplored the death of the Emperor; in another, after announcing the
abolition of the Imperial system and the Restoration of the
Republic, he indicated the manner in which the Government was to be
reconstructed, described the branches into which public authority
was to be divided, and named the Directors.  Attached to the
different documents there appeared the signatures of several
Senators whose names he recollected but with whom he had ceased to
have any intercourse for a great number of years.  . These
signatures were all written by Mallet, and he drew up a decree in
the name of the Senate, and signed by the same Senators, appointing
himself Governor of Paris, and commander of the troops of the first
military division.  He also drew up other decrees in the same form
which purported to promote to higher ranks all the military officers
he intended to make instruments in the execution of his enterprise.
```

The Memoirs of Napoleon, V11, 1812

```
He ordered one regiment to close all the barriers of Paris, and
allow no person to pass through them.  This was done: so that in all
the neighbouring towns from which assistance, in case of need, might
have been obtained, nothing was known of the transactions in Paris.
He sent the other regiments to occupy the Bank, the Treasury, and
different Ministerial offices.  At the Treasury some resistance was
made.  The minister of  that Department was on the spot, and he
employed the guard of his household in maintaining his authority.
But in the whole of the two regiments of the Qnard not a single,
objection was started to the execution of Mallet's orders (Memoirs
of the Duc de Rivogo, tome vi. p. 20.)]—
```

I learned from the porter that the Due de Rovigo had been arrested and carried to the prison of La Force. I went into the house and was informed, to my great astonishment, that the ephemeral Minister was being measured for his official suit, an act which so completely denoted the character of the conspirator that it gave me an insight into the business.

Mallet repaired to General Hulin, who had the command of Paris. He informed him that he had been directed by the Minister of Police to arrest him and seal his papers. Hulin asked to see the order, and then entered his cabinet, where Mallet followed him, and just as Hulin was turning round to speak to him he fired a pistol in his face. Hulin fell: the ball entered his cheek, but the wound was not mortal. The most singular circumstance connected with the whole affair is, that the captain whom Mallet had directed to follow him, and who accompanied him to Hulin's, saw nothing extraordinary in all this, and did nothing to stop it. Mallet next proceeded, very composedly, to Adjutant–General Doucet's. It happened that one of the inspectors of the police was there. He recognised General Mallet as being a man under his supervision. He told him that he had no right to quit the hospital house without leave, and ordered him to be arrested. Mallet, seeing that all was over, was in the act of drawing a pistol from his pocket, but being observed was seized and disarmed. Thus terminated this extraordinary conspiracy, for which fourteen lives paid the forfeit; but, with the exception of Mallet, Guidal, and Lahorie, all the others concerned in it were either machines or dupes.

This affair produced but little effect in Paris, for the enterprise and its result were make known simultaneously. But it was thought droll enough that the Minister and Prefect of Police should be imprisoned by the men who only the day before were their prisoners. Next day I went to see Savary, who had not yet recovered from the stupefaction caused by his extraordinary adventure. He was aware that his imprisonment; though it lasted only half an hour, was a subject of merriment to the Parisians. The Emperor, as I have already mentioned, left Moscow on the day when Mallet made his bold attempt, that is to say, the 19th of October. He was at Smolensko when he heard the news. Rapp, who had been wounded before the entrance into Moscow, but who was sufficiently recovered to return home, was with Napoleon when the latter received the despatches containing an account of what had happened in Paris. He informed me that Napoleon was much agitated on perusing them, and that he launched into abuse of the inefficiency of the police. Rapp added that he did not confine himself to complaints against the agents of his authority. "Is, then, my power so insecure," said he, "that it may be put in peril by a single individual, and a prisoner? It would appear that my crown is not fixed very firmly on my head if in my own capital the bold stroke of three adventurers can shake it. Rapp, misfortune never comes alone; this is the complement of what is passing here. I cannot be everywhere; but I must go back to Paris; my presence there is indispensable to reanimate public opinion. I must have men and money. Great successes and great victories will repair all. I must set off." Such were the motives which induced the Emperor to leave his army. It is not without indignation that I have heard his precipitate departure attributed to personal cowardice. He was a stranger to such feelings, and was never more happy than on the field of battle. I can readily conceive that he was much alarmed on hearing of Mallet's enterprise. The remarks which he made to Rapp were those which he knew would be made by the public, and he well knew that the affair was calculated to banish those illusions of power and stability with which he endeavoured to surround his government.

On leaving Moscow Napoleon consigned the wrecks of his army to the care of his most distinguished generals to Murat who had so ably commanded the cavalry, but who abandoned the army to return to Naples; and to Ney, the hero, rather than the Prince of the Moskowa, whose name will be immortal in the annals of glory, as his death will be eternal in the annals of party revenge. Amidst the general disorder Eugene, more than any other chief, maintained a sort of discipline among the Italians; and it was remarked that the troops of the south engaged in the fatal campaign of Moscow had endured the rigour of the cold better than those troops who were natives of less genial climates.

Napoleon's return from Moscow was not like his returns from the campaigns of Vienna and Tilsit when he came back crowned with laurels, and bringing peace as the reward of his triumphs. It was remarked that Napoleon's first great disaster followed the first enterprise he undertook after his marriage with Maria Louisa. This tended to confirm the popular belief that the presence of Josephine was favourable to his fortune; and superstitious as he sometimes was, I will not venture to affirm that he himself did not adopt this ides. He now threw off even the semblance of legality in the measures of his government: he assumed arbitrary power, under the impression that the critical circumstances in which he was placed would excuse everything. But, however inexplicable were the means to which the Emperor resorted to procure resources, it is but just to acknowledge that they were the consequence of his system of government, and that he evinced inconceivable activity in repairing his losses so as to place himself in a situation to resist his enemies, and restore the triumph of the French standard.

But in spite of all Napoleon's endeavours the disasters of the campaign of Russia were daily more and more sensibly felt. The King of Prussia had played a part which was an acknowledgment of his weakness in joining France, instead of openly declaring himself for the cause of Russia, which was also his. Then took place the defection of General York, who commanded the Prussian contingent to Napoleon's army. The King of Prussia, though no doubt secretly satisfied with the conduct of General York, had him tried and condemned; but shortly after that sovereign commanded in person the troops which had turned against ours. The defection of the Prussians produced a very ill effect, and it was easy to perceive that other defections would follow. Napoleon, foreseeing the fatal chances which this event was likely to draw upon him, assembled a privy council, composed of the Ministers and some of the great officers of his household. MM. de Talleyrand and Cambaceres, and the President of the senate were present. Napoleon asked whether, in the complicated difficulties of our situation, it would be more advisable to negotiate for peace or to prepare for a new war. Cambaceres and Talleyrand gave their opinion in favour of peace, which however, Napoleon would not hear of after a defeat; but the Due de Feltre, —[Clarke]— knowing how to touch the susceptible chord in the mind of Bonaparte, said that he would consider the Emperor dishonoured if he consented to the abandonment of the smallest village which had been united to the Empire by a 'Senatus– consulte'. This opinion was adopted, and the war continued.

On Napoleon's return to Paris the Pope, who was still at Fontainebleau, determined to accede to an arrangement, and to sign an act which the Emperor conceived would terminate the differences between them. But being influenced by some of the cardinals who had previously incurred the Emperor's displeasure Pius VII. disavowed the new Concordat which he had been weak enough to grant, and the Emperor, who then had more important affairs on his hands, dismissed the Holy Father, and published the act to which he had assented. Bonaparte had no leisure to pay attention to the new difficulties started by Pius VII.; his thoughts were wholly directed to the other side of the Rhine. He was unfortunate, and the powers with whom he was most intimately allied separated from him, as he might have expected, and Austria was not the last to imitate the example set by Prussia. In these difficult circumstances the Emperor, who for some time past had observed the talent and address of the Comte Louis de Narbonne, sent him to Vienna, to supersede M. Otto; but the pacific propositions of M. de Narbonne were not listened to. Austria would not let slip the fair opportunity of taking revenge without endangering herself.

Napoleon now saw clearly that since Austria had abandoned him and refused her contingent he should soon have all Europe arrayed against him. But this did not intimidate him.

Some of the Princes of the Confederation of the Rhine still remained faithful to him; and his preparations being completed, he proposed to resume in person the command of the army which had been so miraculously reproduced. But before his departure Napoleon, alarmed at the recollection of Mallet's attempt, and anxious to guard against any similar occurrence during his absence, did not, as on former occasions, consign the reins of the National Government to a Council of Ministers, presided over by the Arch-Chancellor. Napoleon placed my successor with him, M. Meneval, near the Empress Regent as Secretaire des Commandemens (Principal Secretary), and certainly he could not have made a better choice. He made the Empress Maria Louisa Regent, and appointed a Council of Regency to assist her.

```
—[Meneval, who had held the post of Secretary to Napoleon from the
time of Bourrienne's disgrace in 1802, had been nearly killed by the
hardships of the Russian campaign, and now received an honourable
and responsible but less onerous post.  He remained with the Empress
till 7th May 1815, when, finding that she would not return to her
husband, he left her to rejoin his master.]—
```

Printed in the United States
133876LV00003B/96/A